Isabel McNeill Carley Orff Essentials Collection

Making It Up As You Go

SELECTED ESSAYS
Writing About Music,
Improvisation, and Teaching

Isabel McNeill Carley

Copyright © 2011-2023
Brasstown Press
All rights reserved.

B P
Brasstown Press
Charlottesville, VA
brasstownpress.com

Printed in USA
ISBN 978-0-9836545-3-7

Commentary

This collection of twenty-one essays from the pen of one of our most thoughtful pioneers is a landmark publication.

A passionate believer in the Orff Approach, IMC (as she is referred to here) articulates her respect for the compositional excellence represented in the Music for Children Volumes, her strength of belief in Orff process (as opposed to product) and an energetic dedication to "the supreme importance of improvisation." She was a member of the first-ever yearlong intensive training course at the Orff Institute in Salzburg in 1963-64; after that she returned to the USA to become a leader in the North American Orff movement for the next forty years.

The book is divided into three sections: Origins, Practicum, and Exhortations, with some useful reference material in a Resource section at the end. IMC draws attention to the use of many pentatonics in the Schulwerk, including those centred on tones other than doh or lah. She was an advocate for the use of American folk songs featuring many modal, and unusual pentatonic tone sets.

Altogether this is a collection to savour, to dip into and read in bits and pieces, or from cover to cover. It clarifies important, perhaps sometimes overlooked, understandings from the dawn of the development of Orff pedagogy and inspires belief in the model, and its ongoing relevance.

– **Catherine West** in *Ostinato*

Acknowledgments

Thanks to IMC's former colleagues and friends whose encouragement and feedback saw this project through.

Thanks to the American Orff-Schulwerk Association and *The Orff Echo*, as well as Orff Canada Music for Children / Musique pour Enfants and *Ostinato* for permissions to re-use previously published materials.

Note on this edition
This book retains all the positive traits of its underlying materials. Inconsistencies and errors are the responsibility of its editor. Special thanks to JWS.

Edited and produced by Brasstown Press with production assistance from Ayla Palermo. Cover art by Browning Porter Design. Printed in USA.

Memorable Quotations

Play is the basis of all art
– Anonymous

From Isabel McNeill Carley

- The emphasis is on playing with the materials of music, on developing musical ideas, just as a composer does. In this way, music comes alive as an immediate and stimulating activity for children. Their participation and their own ideas are being explored and developed. That is why it's so important to include real choices for the children – and for the teacher, too.

- I have attempted to construct a new kind of [American] curriculum, one that keeps repeating key activities, but with a difference each time. [This means] new suggestions, new demands, new contexts, new combinations of movement, of speech, song and accompaniments, using body percussion, unpitched percussion, and one or two bar instruments – whatever seems appropriate and the class is ready to play with.

- The cultivation of taste depends on making choices. In my experience, students of any age can reach this stage of playing creatively with the materials of music only when they're comfortable with the material, the assignment, and the class environment.

And

- Don't practice in public.

- No one ever improvises beyond his or her ability.

- An ostinato is not a phrase. It goes on and on, camouflaging the phrase breaks.

- No holes in the carpet!

- [Too much]emphasis on the curriculum can omit essential elements, like a heavy diet sans salads or fruits.

- Human beings need both repetition and novelty.

- In play, no one knows the outcome. The experience is different for every participant.

- In improvisation there's no Winner, no Star. Volunteer. Solo, or lose yourself in the crowd; everything's essential.

- *Ausgezeichnet!*

Making It Up As You Go

CONTENTS

Editor's Note / Schulwerk Terms
Glossary
Introduction

Part One • Origins

1	The Orff Approach	1
2	On Changing Your Life	13
3	Studies in Salzburg	16
4	AOSA Beginnings and The Orff Echo	20
5	Gunild Keetman, In Appreciation	23
6	The Magic Carpet of Sound	29
7	The Musical Realm of the Pentatonic	31

Part Two • Practicum

8	Where Then Do We Begin?	45
9	Speech Play: Theory and Practice	49
10	Building the Layered Orff Ensemble	67
11	The Essential Use of Improvisation in Teaching Recorder	70
12	Hand Drums: Playing Techniques and Repertoire	79
13	Music Plus: Kindergarten Curriculum Goals	86
14	Advice to Orff Teachers	89
15	Transformations	94

Part Three • Exhortations

16	Training: Once Is Never Enough	99
17	Music Worth the Difference	102
18	Ersatz Orff (And How To Avoid It)	104
19	On Teaching Styles	107
20	The Value of Side Trips	110
21	Create or Perform?	113

Resources

Biographical Sketch – Isabel McNeill Carley	117
Music & Instructional Works by IMC	118
Brasstown Press Catalogue	121

Editor's Note

The essays and articles selected here, both published and unpublished, have never before been assembled or coordinated. Some themes and threads revealed themselves, and we used them to organize the book's contents. We decided to revise, emend, and correct with a light touch, to leave the original texts to speak for themselves.

The previously published articles that *The Orff Echo* and Orff Canada's *Ostinato* graciously granted permission to reprint have been only slightly edited in most instances. All the music notation has been reset; otherwise the overall tone, form, and opinions of the originals are unaltered.

Any introduced inaccuracies or errors are, of course, solely the responsibility of the editor.

Schulwerk Terms

Schulwerk, a German word meaning something like "school [music] pieces," has become a general American term among Orff teachers and enthusiasts for the teachings and music education resources conceived and created by Carl Orff and Gunild Keetman, or inspired by them. This may also be referred to as "Orff-Schulwerk," which sometimes refers more narrowly to Orff books and printed publications, collectively.

Note, throughout this book, "Volume" or "Vol" or "Vols" with a Roman numeral refers exclusively to the volumes of *Orff-Schulwerk: Music for Children*, Margaret Murray's English (UK) adaptation of the German original. Occasionally, this is also referred to as the "Murray Edition." There are two other adaptations in English, the Hall/Walter version which is referred to but not specifically cited in this book, and the "American Edition," a three-volume work based on the original *Orff-Schulwerk: Musik für Kinder*, but heavily revised with American music pieces, edited by Hermann Regner of the Orff Institute.

Glossary

Bar instruments • General term applied to the Orff Instrumentarium of removable-bar pitched percussion played with mallets – glockenspiels (higher pitched metal bars), xylophones (resonant wooden bars), metallophones (resonant metal bars, lower pitched and with longer tone decay than glockenspiels).

Bordun • Simple drone accompaniment, typically using tonic and/or fifth only.

Carley, Isabel McNeill (1918-2011) • Canadian-American educator, author and composer. First American honors graduate of the Orff-Institute (1964), a founder of the American Orff-Schulwerk Association (1968), founding editor of *The Orff Echo* (1968-1983).

Carley, James Rea (1909-2004) • American composer. Professor of Church Music at Christian Theological Seminary, Indianapolis, Indiana (1953-1973).

Elementaria: First Acquaintance with Orff-Schulwerk • Gunild Keetman's distilling into one book the entire philosophy and learning sequence for the Orff Approach.

Gestalt • (German) The entirety. Gestalt psychology takes a holistic view of the brain, perception, and learning.

Güntherschule • Founded in 1924 by Dorothee Günther and Carl Orff in Munich, Germany, it was a college-level school for gymnastic education, elementary music, and modern dance. Closed by the Nazis in 1944, it was destroyed by Allied bombing in 1945. Gunild Keetman, after completing her studies there in 1929, began working as a teacher at the school with Carl Orff. They developed the pedagogy and musical approaches there that were to become the Orff-Schulwerk.

Keetman, Gunild (1904-1990) • German dancer, musician, composer and educator. Co-founded the Orff Approach to music education.

Montessori, Maria (1870-1952) • Italian physician and founder of the influential philosophy of Montessori childhood education, in which instructors encourage children's innate abilities.

Mozarteum • In Salzburg, Austria, it was the first home of the Orff-Institute, which it still sponsors. Founded in the Nineteenth Century, it became a university for the arts in 1998.

Making It Up As You Go

Murray, Margaret (1921-) • English educator, musician, and composer who translated and adapted the Schulwerk Volumes into English. She also founded the Orff Society UK. In her Volumes, which were published from 1959 to 1965, she included many English and Scottish rhymes, sayings, and folk songs. These volumes are still widely used in Canada and the United States in Orff teacher training courses and classrooms.

Orff, Carl (1895-1982) • German composer and co-founder, with his former student, Gunild Keetman, of the Orff-Schulwerk approach to music education.

Orff-Institut / Orff Institute • In Salzburg, Austria, it was established in 1961, its building opened 1963. Provides definitive training for teachers of Orff-Schulwerk.

Ostinato • A repeating rhythmic pattern (from the Italian word for stubborn or obstinate). Plural, "ostinati."

Patschen • (German) Rhythmical knee-slapping. Used in the Orff Approach as one of the body percussion instruments (finger snaps, claps, patschen, stamps). Has taken on common usage in English. One knee-slap is known in English as a "patsch."

Paralipomena • Greek for "leftovers," the German Schott publication (1966) is a follow-up to the five Volumes of the Orff-Schulwerk.

Piaget, Jean (1896-1980) • The French-speaking, Swiss psychologist and philosopher known for his developmental studies of children. He strongly favored a more child-centered approach to education and greatly influenced European and American educators.

Schott Music • Originally based in Mainz, Germany, one of the world's leading music publishers since 1770.

Steiner, Rudolf (1861-1925) • Austrian philosopher, architect, and educational reformer. Developed Eurhythmy and the Waldorf School educational approach.

The "Volumes" • A five-book series, numbered I – V, constituting the foundational sources for study and practice of Orff-Schulwerk. The Volumes were published first in German (Carl Orff – Gunild Keetman: *Orff-Schulwerk Musik für Kinder*) and then in English (Carl Orff – Gunild Keetman: *Orff-Schulwerk Music for Children, English Version adapted by Margaret Murray*).

Introduction

This collection of written pieces by my mother is interesting to me – and I hope to many others – for its depth of appreciation of the Orff Schulwerk. These essays are in effect her long valentine to Carl Orff and to Gunild Keetman, particularly. The less well known of the two co-founders, Keetman devoted herself to developing and communicating the "Orff Approach."

I recall my mother speaking of Keetman's extreme shyness. She once told my mother that she had no interest in having the Orff Schulwerk named for her. It would have made her uncomfortable. Keetman wielded her influence more directly, if subtly. First through the Orff Approach itself, then in the music she wrote and the arrangements she conceived, and ultimately with the many students, including my mother, whom she inspired.

In compiling this Isabel McNeill Carley collection, I came to understand through her writings two things more clearly than ever. One, that Orff and Keetman treated the five main Schulwerk Volumes – and others that preceded and followed – as serious compositional challenges. This may be obvious, but in the context of childhood music education, perhaps not so expected. Two, that by combining early European music (from the time before functional cadential harmony reigned supreme) with Indonesian layered melodic patterns, African layered percussive ostinati, and their own creative musical process, they synthesized for the world a great gift.

Beyond IMC's appreciation of the founders of the Orff movement, we see her curiosity about and basic understanding of how humans learn. She passionately wanted to bring to life her students' innate abilities. Always thirsty for the latest news in psychological research, she looked for facts and theories to substantiate her intuitions about the crucial role speech plays, the supreme importance of improvisation, and the value of demonstrations of works-in-progress, rather than canned, staged performances. She conducted an ongoing quest to reach people and open their lives to more music. She jotted down quotations from experts in the sciences – aerospace, physics, psychology, linguistics, anthropology. She searched her own experiences as a child and as a teacher of children and young adults to gather nuggets of wisdom and insight. (And she never stopped collecting pentatonic folk songs.)

My father's generosity made all this possible. Well along in his teaching career, he was awarded his first sabbatical. He wanted to study composition during the 1963-64 academic year. That was exactly when the Orff Institute would open its new building on Salzburg's Frohnburgweg and admit students for a yearlong intensive training course. (Also, for what it's worth, it was the year they were filming exterior shots for *The Sound of Music* at the Schloss next door.) So he stepped aside, offering the year to his wife. It was the career-changing opportunity of her lifetime. She never forgot that act of love.

Making It Up As You Go

Three of us moved to Salzburg in the fall of 1963. My two older siblings were in college. But as I was just recently reminded, IMC already had overcome another hurdle, to persuade Admissions that forty-five wasn't too old to attend. She was accepted and did just fine. By the following summer she was teaching at Orff courses in the US, and the momentum kept building from there, for she had found her calling. She retired from teaching more than forty years later.

Many years ago, for three consecutive summers, I was a junior instructor with her at Barbara Grenoble's University of Denver summer Orff certification courses. While I enjoyed working with the classroom teachers who had little or no musical training, IMC particularly liked to engage with the students who were experienced musicians or were otherwise unafraid of a challenge. Her own confidence rarely seemed in question.

In the 1940s and 50s she had put together her ideas on early childhood music, speech, and movement, and later tested them in her private piano lessons and preschool music classes – some of which I attended and still remember. Then Keetman and Orff and the crew provided a context she was seeking, and with the tools of the Orff Approach, she forged a new foundation for her life's work with children and adults.

I hope this new book, along with the three **Recorder Improvisation and Technique** books we are re-issuing along with it, can preserve and continue her work for generations to come. (Visit brasstownpress.com for more.)

Anne M Carley
Charlottesville, VA

Part One

Origins

I shall never forget my first encounter with Gunild Keetman. Both of us had gone to the University of Toronto campus to get the lay of the land and to check out the building where we would be meeting the next morning. She walked slightly ahead of me. I was too shy to speak out, yet we were very much aware of each other as we continued our explorations.

    IMC in "On Changing Your Life"

Making It Up As You Go

1. The Orff Approach

The Orff Approach is a new and vastly innovative way of teaching music to children. It is named after Carl Orff (1895-1982), the famous German composer of *Carmina Burana, Der Mond, Die Kluge, Antigonae,* and other works. He and Gunild Keetman, his lifelong associate, originally worked out these methods with young adult students in the late 1920s. Associated "Orff-Schulwerk" publications first appeared in the 1930s. Revised and recast as radio school lessons for younger children in the late 1940s, these were expanded and published in the 1950s in a definitive German edition, the well-known five-volume *Orff-Schulwerk: Musik für Kinder.* Another volume, *Paralipomena,* was added in 1966.

Not until the late 1960s were all five volumes available in an English (UK) adaptation by Margaret Murray. (Separately, a truncated English translation with added materials by Doreen Hall and Arnold Walter had been issued in the 1950s for American and Canadian students.) In the late 1970s a new three-book American Edition, edited by Hermann Regner and reorganized with predominantly American materials, was published. All of these works, along with various supplements and more than fifteen foreign-language versions, are part of a rich treasure trove of basic resources available to us since the 1980s. Pre-eminent among these is Keetman's book, *Elementaria: First Acquaintance with Orff-Schulwerk,* a concise step-by-step guide to the entire progression of the Orff Approach.

WHAT IS IT?

The Orff Approach combines singing, movement and instrumental play. It is based on speech and the natural movement that any normal, untrained human can do spontaneously. Children are introduced to a new ensemble of specially designed instruments with beautiful tone – xylophones, glockenspiels, and metallophones of different ranges, requiring only large muscle movements to play. Standard percussion instruments of excellent quality are added in: drums, cymbals, triangles, woodblocks, tambourines, *etc*. Voices, recorders, and a bass provided by cello, gamba, guitar or timpani round out the ensemble.

Music making precedes music reading, as it did historically, and as it still does in children's play. The emphasis is on participation and discovery, not on the performance of set pieces for an audience The reward is in the doing. The Orff instruments lend themselves to accompanying and solo work, are amazingly versatile, and have a magical sound that opens children's ears to first experience the joy of ensemble playing. Most of all, they encourage musical play, discovery, and improvisation.

Significantly, music making never is meant to stand alone, but always arises in conjunction with speech and movement. Influenced by Émile Jaques-Dalcroze of the previous generation, who pioneered eurhythmics, Orff put movement training right alongside music learning. For him, speech, music, and movement originate together. Paradoxically, the movement aspect, in particular, is neglected in the five central Orff-Schulwerk volumes, probably because the books were derived from radio programs that obviously could not show movement exercises – and perhaps also because movement notation is so generally inadequate and rhythmic training so difficult to describe.

Muscles are slow to learn, but muscular freedom is basic to any music making. This is plainly in line with Orff's own interest in musical theater, where speech, rhythm, melody, movement, and instruments are all united by the composer's design. Orff held that music is an inclusive art, as it was in classical Greece, as it remains today among peoples with unadulterated folk traditions, and as it always has been in children's play. It is in speech and play – music in the most basic sense

---

*Carl Orff, in "The Schulwerk – Its Origin and Aims," University of Toronto, 1962, a 24-page booklet authored by Carl Orff and prepared for the July, 1962 Toronto conference. It has been anthologized subsequently in several collections.

– that the student begins. From here the Orff Approach can show the way to deeper musical knowledge and personal accomplishment.

HOW WAS IT DEVISED?

"Our pieces were not first written out and afterwards performed. They were extemporizations. After much playing some might be set in notation. Reading was rather uncommon; the music was learnt by heart and played from memory."*

Orff shared with his contemporaries a profound interest in so-called "primitive" cultures and the fresh ideas in education and the arts that swept across Europe in the wake of World War I. The inadequate training of the theater musicians he was then working with spurred him to experiments in music education. In 1924, he founded a new school in Munich with Dorothee Günther, the Güntherschule for rhythmic education, adopting her maxim, "From movement, music – from music, dance."

This is where "Orff instruments" first debuted. They answered the need for simple ensemble instruments on which students could improvise their own music to accompany movement and dance. The percussion instruments were generally of the usual sort, but the bar instruments were newly devised, although based on Medieval and global examples. Of different ranges, they were designated as xylophones, metallophones, and glockenspiels, and joined a more familiar group of recorders, bass instruments like kettledrums, string instruments and guitars.

In 1930 the first version of Schulwerk publications began production with the help of Gunild Keetman. These small books provided basic technique and repertoire for each family of instruments and some instrumental ensembles. Orff later noted: "The old Schulwerk had addressed itself to an older age group, to prospective teachers of movement and dance. As it stood it was not applicable to children." The Güntherschule and most of the original instruments were destroyed during World War II. It was not until 1949 that Orff again turned to music education, when he agreed to do a few programs for children on Bavarian Radio. These programs, under the direction of Gunild Keetman, elicited such an enthusiastic response that they continued for five years.

The world-famous second edition of the Schulwerk volumes followed, substantially a record of these radio programs, but organized and amplified to present a comprehensive plan for basic music education. The firm Schott Music published the five German volumes from 1950-55. (They were also the original publishers of Carl Orff's compositions.) Today, Orff and Keetman's *Music for Children*, as it is known in its English adaptation, remains the essential resource, musically and pedagogically, for teachers of the Orff Approach.

Their great work is not, however, a systematic method, in spite of its logical arrangement and development. It may be tempting to view the five volumes as a curriculum for five school years, but that would be far off the mark. The Orff Approach's multifaceted, experiential nature defies printed presentation, reading as we must one step at a time. In actual practice, music and movement and speech and song must grow together simultaneously.

There is, for instance, no general guide to the use of movement in any of the Orff-Schulwerk volumes, beyond the inclusion of exercises for body percussion and occasional body percussion parts notated in individual pieces. Admittedly, it is hard to reduce movement to words, yet too many teachers will omit this aspect entirely. Their justification is likely the similar omission from the Schulwerk volumes, but to omit movement from the Orff classroom is a serious mistake.

Keep in mind what the five volumes are and are not. They are certainly a record of what was done with a group of children over a period of five years, a model of what can be achieved, and a guide for creative teachers who want to enrich their classes with the same kind of total immersion in music. Equally importantly, this is not a pedagogical bible, a be-all and end-all, nor did Orff and Keetman ever suggest it was.

USING THE ORFF APPROACH CREATIVELY

A teacher who wants to use the Orff Approach must know at least these volumes thoroughly, and then work backward and forward in them. The teacher will use speech and rhythm exercises, technical instrument exercises, songs and instrumental pieces. The teacher will use movement to reinforce rhythmic training, to develop muscular freedom, and to clarify musical form. The teacher will never neglect the improvisation training which is basic to the whole approach. From the simplest beginnings in speech and movement, musical vocabulary and technique develop over the five volumes. Through chant, percussion play, native and foreign folk songs, folk dances, and instrumental pieces, students are ultimately led to highly sophisticated settings of texts from the Bible and Goethe's *Faust*. The materials of music have been gradually and logically introduced.

The pentatonic (Volume I) is followed by major modes (Volumes II and III) and minor modes (Volumes IV and V), first with bordun (drone) accompaniments, then with moving borduns and ostinati, and later with shifting chords. Notice the emphasis throughout the first four volumes on the many varieties of modal music. Cadential harmony is broached only after this long development, as was the historical case in Western music. (See also the section on Monodic Style below for a fuller description.)

With the Orff Approach, the emphasis is not on the development of skilled performance by a few, but on the participation by all on many levels at once. There is a balance of solo and ensemble work from the beginning, and everyone can contribute at his or her own level. Participation does not depend on reading ability, but on listening. Not surprisingly to Orff teachers, technique develops fastest through spontaneous musical play, improvisation, and ensemble playing, as pupils begin to *think* music.

Caught up in the ensemble experience, students willingly invest tremendous concentration to stay together, to hear the other parts, to learn their own and to play by heart. Music notation is introduced only after a common vocabulary has been built up by ear, and only when children want to know how to write down their improvisations to play again later. Most important, the message is that music is to be enjoyed. As it is made. As it grows in the classroom. As it is renewed with each improvisation. Music is not something only to be prepared for a future audience, drilled and polished until the life has gone out of it. That is the antithesis of the Orff Approach. Orff and Keetman wanted to share with children the joy of making music.

WHAT'S NEW ABOUT IT?

Progressive music teachers have been working to bring music alive in their classrooms in many ways for a good many years. Movement, singing, dramatic play, classroom instruments, listening, music reading, and creative projects have all been introduced at one time or another to further this educational vision. What, then, is different about the Orff Approach?

Yes, the visionary goal is similar but the Orff Approach emphasis is decidedly new. What does a modern child need to learn to be an intelligent listener, a competent amateur musician, or even a composer? Or alternatively, what are the true concerns of music education? The Orff answer, in part: making and thinking music; weighing different possibilities and choosing what sounds best; working out accompaniments; writing musical introductions, interludes, finished pieces, and simple dances that clarify musical forms.

This is music education taking a composer's point of view, an approach not tied to one single period or one tradition. The aim is to understand and perform music of any style, of any period, of any tradition. It can be as relevant in Japan as in Bavaria, in Brazil as in Greece, in Sweden as America. Such a successful education is not dependent on reading ability or mastering advanced technique, but on fostering innate musicality and building fundamentals like increased aural discrimination and muscular control. The repertoire is deliberately limited to what can be improvised or learned by rote and played by heart.

Orff himself claimed only three distinctive points for his approach:

1. The use of speech as the basis for rhythm training and for singing.
2. The development and introduction of melodic percussion instruments specifically designed for children to first experience the joy of ensemble music making.
3. The emphasis on improvisation.

From my teaching experience, I recognize two additional points:

4. The essential use of body rhythms and movement.
5. The systematic development of a highly sophisticated monodic style that is appealingly global, and not distinctly Western.

Note particularly that Orff's first point is the use of speech. Why should music education begin with speech? Speech exercises develop a feeling for diction, for inflection, for tone color, for phrasing, for rhythmic precision, and for form – all basic to further musical comprehension and the playing of instruments. Even the more advanced musical concepts, such as ostinato and canon, can be usefully introduced through speech, as language is the accustomed tool that students are mastering in school. More fundamentally, words are first used because their sound and rhythm are innate to us all. Spoken words are also a very useful mnemonic device, whereas rhythm patterns alone can easily be forgotten without far too much drill.

MORE ABOUT THE INSTRUMENTS

Recorders are indispensable. It is essential that the teacher play the recorder competently, for it is invaluable in improvisation.

The Orff student ensemble includes three families of similarly constructed barred instruments: glockenspiels, xylophones, and metallophones, each with a distinctive timbre. Glockenspiels are high and bright, like small bells. They are chosen both to play melodies and to add to the ensemble color. Xylophones sound rich and hollow. They are the backbone of the ensemble. Metallophones have light metal bars with a surprisingly long reverberation. They are best used in sustained, slow-moving parts.

In the following list of ranges, bar instruments marked ** are immediately essential, those marked * should be added next, and those marked † are optional but will fully round out the ensemble's sound.

†Bass Xylophone	**Alto Xylophone	*Soprano Xylophone	**Alto Glockenspiel	*Soprano Glockenspiel
†Bass Metallophone	*Alto Metallophone	†Soprano Metallophone		

Soprano and bass metallophones are luxuries to be added, I suggest, only after more alto and soprano xylophones and glockenspiels have been obtained to fill out the ensemble. (Individual metal or wooden bars mounted over a resonating box, from bass to soprano range, are also available to fill in if the budget limits are tight.) Supplementary instrumentation includes small timpani and/or cello, gamba, or duobass. Good-quality percussion instruments are always a necessity: drums of different sizes, triangles, cymbals, woodblocks, tambourines, and jingle bells.

WHY THESE INSTRUMENTS?

The bar instruments have a number of advantages. They are played with large muscle movements that children can master before tackling harder finger dexterity problems on more sophisticated instruments. Aural memory is cultivated, since these instruments almost have to be played by heart. (The basic playing technique alternates hands.) They lend themselves to immediate ensemble playing because of their simplicity, while sensitivity to sound and the differences of timbre and of range are reinforced. And they make a magical "Klang-complex" sound texture that every child is quick to recognize and enjoy.

As Orff intended, the bar instruments can do double duty as accompanying and solo instruments. They encourage improvisation because of their relatively uncomplicated technique and physical construction with removable bars, allowing tonal limits to be reset or expanded as the student's playing skill and imagination grow. They also provide a needed bridge between rhythm instruments and more highly developed melody instruments such as the recorder or cello or the more conventional instruments of our day. Children and musical adults find the combination of timbres uniquely appealing. It is impossible to make ugly noises with them, and even the simplest pattern adds an extra dimension to the simplest song. They are suited to accompanying singers and to playing independent instrumental pieces, with parts that vary greatly in difficulty from easy, open bass drones to technically tricky solo parts for xylophones and glockenspiels.

Whichever Orff instruments are played, the larger achievement is immediate music making. The children do not spend hours fighting to get some sort of musical tone out of their instruments. Anyone who has watched a beginner struggle with a violin or trumpet or flute knows what can happen. By contrast, in the Orff ensemble every member of the class is needed, and makes a real contribution whatever the individual levels of achievement. Yet there is always a challenge for even the most accomplished pupil – and for the teacher. The discipline of ensemble work transforms the slower learners, and due to the concentration required, all their schoolwork may benefit from this musical training. Most heartening to teachers, the class may grant new respect to a child who, for instance, can improvise unusually well, or is particularly imaginative and skillful in movement, or is very quick to memorize a difficult part.

A FEW MORE WORDS ABOUT MONODIC STYLE

In Orff's music, there's no missing the distinctive sound textures where the rhythms and melody dominate. This music is not harmonic in the usual sense, but is instead related to historic musical forms from the Western tradition, and to age-old Indonesian and African models. Many different modal scales are used, not just the familiar major and minor standard scales, which alone are adaptable to conventional harmonic treatment.

In *Music for Children*, simple tunes are built up with the repetition and contrast of accompanying drones and ostinati. Drones, or "borduns" as Orff called them, are sustained open fifths or octaves. With time, the drones may be transformed into rhythmic patterns, instead of being simply sustained or repeated. As technique develops, the bordun tones can be shifted away from the original pitches into what Orff dubbed a "moving bordun." Ostinati, in distinction, are stubborn rhythmic and/or melodic figures that repeat cyclically underneath the primary tune.

On a structural level, parallel movement – paraphony – is used in preference to the contrary movement of the polyphonic period, or the cadential movement of traditional

Western harmony. Essentially, there is one tune, even with all the rhythmic tension and incidental polyphony that the use of ostinati creates. Whether the scale is pentatonic, modal, major, or minor, the Orff style remains constantly engaging. In a larger context, *Music for Children* not only teaches real respect for the characteristics of different scales, but it also champions the poetic quality of language, the imaginative use of timbre, and the musical possibilities of percussion ensembles. The choice of texts is unequalled in schoolroom music. It's also noteworthy that in spite of the Central European heritage of both Orff and Keetman, it isn't peculiarly German, or even Western. Instead, it is deliberately limited to what is *basic* in the art of music, making it universal.

CRITICISM OF THE ORFF APPROACH

Ardent apologists, and even more ardent critics, have written much on the Orff Approach, with misunderstandings on all sides. The field of music education has been highly conservative historically – and in some cases still resembles the Nineteenth-Century European conservatory. Critics, unsurprisingly, have jumped to negative conclusions on the basis of perhaps one (unsuccessful?) demonstration, without stopping to find out what is being proposed.

Many well-trained musicians seem to bristle even at the name, sensing a threat to the status quo and the investment they have made in their own educations and careers. They are right. The Orff Approach does challenge their assumptions. But many creative teachers think it's high time! Why should music alone still be tied to the tastes, knowledge, and traditional expectations of the mid Nineteenth-Century middle class? Think of the recent changes in teaching art, languages, science and math. [As I write this,] we've been in the Twentieth Century a long time already. Surely it is time to start taking seriously the new ideas that Carl Orff began to work out as far back as the 1920s.

Too often, people who meet Orff's ideas for the first time assume that the simple pentatonic song arrangements and instrumental pieces from Volume I, with which teachers and children always need to begin, represent the entire Orff Approach. But they think you must proceed literally, following the printed page like mesmerized deer without even a nod to the improvisation and movement that the Schulwerk was designed to stimulate. In reality this is only the beginning, and only a pale suggestion.

Orff himself said time after time that music does not stand alone. Always it should be combined with speech, with song, with movement, with percussion, with pitched instruments – with everything that makes music a part of life.

This is a tall order. It is not the sort of thing one learns in two weeks, no matter how much previous training and personal experience a teacher may bring to it. Frankly, the Orff Approach is not as easy as it looks to the outsider or neophyte. Let me condense Werner Thomas's assessment from his article on the Schulwerk in "Carl Orff, A Report in Words and Pictures":

> *Das Schulwerk* is ... not a method but rather a revelation of a mature world of language and sound....[I]n the light of history [Orff] thus identifies his pedagogical practice with the evolution of the Western intellect....[It] is no pedagogical construction but an historical crystallization. [From Schott 1960 edition]

EIGHT KEY VALUES OF THE ORFF APPROACH

1. It provides incomparable rhythmic training.
2. Ensemble music-making is emphasized from the very beginning, on real instruments with beautiful tone that are designed for children and require minimal technique.
3. It restores music to its historic position as an essential discipline in education and a humanizing influence, since both group cooperation and individual creativity are cultivated and valued. Each individual contributes at his or her own level; each person's contribution is needed and appreciated.
4. Music is no longer isolated and exploited as a skill, but allied with all the creative arts and with integrated learning.
5. Children discover for themselves how music is made – by making it. They learn how music developed historically by actually using historical techniques. They learn to think music and to judge for themselves. They are equipped to follow their own path whether that leads to early music, contemporary music, jazz, blues, pop, world music, or the more standard fare of private lessons and classical concerts.
6. Improvisation is the heart of the Orff Approach, improvisation in speech, in rhythm, in melody, in accompaniment, in movement, and in teaching itself. Music comes alive in the classroom. New ways of teaching explore improvisation, bringing creativity into the music period, day after day.
7. Concentration and creativity are cultivated and encouraged, and are transferable to other subjects. All education benefits, not just the music program. The choice of rhymes, folk songs, poems, and prose texts can spark a vital appreciation of each student's own cultural heritage. The progression from the simplest play chants of Volume I to the settings of texts from Goethe and the Bible at the end of Volume V creates what Orff terms a common "intellectual humus" to nourish further growth.

8. It is accessible to everyone – normal, handicapped, or emotionally disturbed students, bright and slow learners, readers and non-readers, and teachers without formal music training – because it is based on our shared human, pre-intellectual musical impulses. For the first time, classroom teachers can teach music with confidence and freedom, since they no longer need to demonstrate complex musical skills like piano playing. With their pupils, teachers are free to follow and cultivate their own musical impulses as far as they can go.

THE CHALLENGE AND PROMISE FOR TEACHERS

To teachers, I say, "Don't be discouraged."

It is challenging to use or teach from any of the Schulwerk books as they stand. In *Music for Children*, materials are included at different levels throughout each volume. Arrangements must often be simplified for primary children, and texts changed to appeal to older children. As a teacher, you must be jumping to and fro, if you are going to include speech and rhythm exercises, technical instrumental exercises, song arrangements and instrumental pieces.

In addition, there is no hint of how to approach movement training, nor is there explicit instruction in improvisation in the books themselves. This you will have to learn from live courses, supplementary works, and most importantly your own personal experience. The Volumes aren't directly concerned with teaching notation and music reading, either, although Orff states very clearly that such instruction should be parallel to the use of *Music for Children* from the beginning. Take heart, though, as you will find the scores *look* far more complicated than they really are.

Turning to what other English versions offer, even the Hall and Walter adaptation contains only a handful of American rhymes and songs, while the Murray Edition relies on English and Scottish examples. Yet again take heart, for our own American musical heritage is infinitely richer. The three American Edition books provide inspiring examples of the variety we enjoy here. Compared to Orff's Bavarian tradition, we have a wealth of pentatonic and modal tunes. We have cowboy songs, Spirituals, blues, Native American songs. We have play songs and work songs in the pentatonic modes – and unlike the *Musik für Kinder* volumes, not just in C pentatonic. We have echo songs and question and answer songs, especially out of the African-American "call and response" tradition, and we have sea chanteys. And we have a living tradition of modal tunes, largely from the Appalachians, that is still passed down generation to generation. We are heirs to all these songs and folk traditions that succeeding waves of immigrants brought with them. This collection of songs from Europe, from Africa, from Asia, from Central and South

America is a vaster legacy than any other culture in the world. Remember that Orff and Keetman, for lack of German folk materials, had to invent pentatonic tunes for the Schulwerk, and either compose or borrow modal pieces from other European traditions. We have our own suitable songs in great abundance. The Orff Approach and Orff-Schulwerk are a great boon to teachers of music everywhere. But it is with our own that music education in America should proceed.

This essay was previously unpublished. It was written c. 1980.

2. On Changing Your Life

I shall never forget my first encounter with Gunild Keetman. It was in Toronto in the summer of 1962, the evening before the first Orff Conference and courses in North America. Both of us had gone to the University of Toronto campus to get the lay of the land and to check out the building where we would be meeting the next morning. She walked slightly ahead of me. I was too shy to speak out, yet we were very much aware of each other as we continued our explorations.

Earlier, I'd seen several provocative articles about the "Orff Approach" in professional magazines. Two German friends in Chicago had shown me the first two volumes of the German edition of *Musik für Kinder* and also let me doodle on the alto xylophone and metallophone they'd brought back from abroad. With no notion of how to proceed further, I was ready and waiting when the Toronto conclave was announced. Immediately, I decided to go. I was attracted to the course by the opportunity to find out about the whole approach directly from Orff and his colleagues, since what little I'd seen was definitely *not* self-explanatory. Also the emphasis on ensemble in the Orff Approach from the beginning seemed like sound psychology, to me, since it's always more fun making music with other people than doing it alone.

I rode up to Toronto from Indianapolis with Candace Ramsay, who was then teaching Music Education at Ball State in Muncie, Indiana. At my next encounter with Keetman at the conference, I somehow had the temerity to give her a copy of my just-issued first book of piano pieces for children, *Eleven Miniatures*. The next day, she stopped me in the hall to say that she and Dr. Orff thought my pieces ideal for children!

The conference proved extraordinarily stimulating. Standout events were Professor Keller's classes in arranging and composition in the Orff style, with repertoire from Volumes II, III, and IV. Keller gave us advanced students a taste of repertoire and techniques well beyond the introductory level, so we were able to get a wider view of the whole approach. I remember writing my first Orff arrangement, a setting of Richard Chase's version of **Cock Robin**, and reading through and analyzing pieces from my brand-new Orff-Schulwerk books.

The Recorder Ensemble sessions with Arnie Grayson, Mimi Samuelson, Isabel Shack, and a good bass player from Montreal were outstanding. I'd never encountered really good players before, so it was a singular treat. I was also quite taken with Dr. Orff's lecture-demonstration. He included recorded examples of Orff-Schulwerk repertoire by Margaret Murray's children in England, using examples of body percussion, speech play, songs and dances from the first three volumes – the first opportunity to hear Orff repertoire actually performed by children. (Later there were demonstrations by Lois Birkenshaw's students and others as well.) Dr. Walter's stimulating lecture about the background and importance of the Orff Approach was later reprinted in *Orff Re-Echoes I*, a valuable resource.

Dr. Richard Johnston's stunning lecture-demonstration used many of our North American limited-range folk songs and rhymes as convincing examples of what could be brought into the Orff Approach. (He contrasted this to what he referred to as the "gapped major" scale as used in Volume I.) Johnston's sessions underlined the need to study, analyze and collect relevant folk material from our own traditions – which I started to do as soon as I got home, building an appropriate pentatonic repertoire for my own classes. (Let me suggest that you do likewise, or at least order Louise Bradford's wonderful collection of American pentatonic songs entitled *Sing It Yourself* as an inexhaustible resource.) Orff and Keetman did set us a bad example, by inventing all the pentatonic songs in Volume I, but they had good reason, since there is no tradition of pentatonic song in Western Europe (except in Scotland and Ireland). And Orff was a great composer, as most of us are not.

In Gunild Keetman's general session she suddenly asked for volunteers to improvise on the recorder. No one responded for what seemed a long time. Then my friend Candace whispered, "Let's do it," and before I knew what was happening, there we were up on the stage in front of this huge crowd. Keetman asked us to improvise to the C-F tetrachord, without any accompaniment at all. We obliged in Question-and-Answer form, ending on F, and the crowd applauded our temerity. Keetman said quietly that she'd hoped we would use D as the tonal center. So at my first brush with this great teacher, I learned that the obvious is only the beginning.

The final session of the conference was the most memorable of all. Carl Orff read aloud his folk play *Astutuli* to an audience of about three hundred American and Canadian music teachers. Few understood German – let alone a medieval Bavarian dialect – but all enjoyed it enormously because of the magical use of his speaking voice. He assumed different roles, playing with the "tune" and tempo of each word. Dr. Orff's presentation hit me as a revelation of the possibilities of musical speech, bringing to vivid life the inner meaning of language.

At the end, Keetman gave the whole audience an unforgettable experience. She led the entire group from all over North America in a C-Pentatonic vocal improvisation, while she played recorder above us. Like me, these were people – kindergarten teachers, classroom teachers, a few full-time mothers, music teacher specialists – who had been waiting for an opportunity to find out about the Orff Approach. We came from elementary schools, colleges, graduate schools. Keetman gave us no rules or talk of form, of solo and group, of question-and-answer, except we were to stay in the pentatonic. With that the hall burst into song, following Keetman's gestures tentatively at first, then with growing delight and confidence.

Imagine, making music together with no notes to decode, no instructions, nothing to distract and hamper us. Just our ears and our voices – our instruments – and her beat to guide us. For me, that was the decisive moment. I knew that this was what I wanted to do with the rest of my life. To make music that involved the play of language, the beauty and accessibility of the ensemble of instruments, and that elusive element I'd already been pursuing in my own teaching – Improvisation.

So I've been at it ever since.

This essay was previously unpublished.

3. Studies in Salzburg

My husband Jim had an academic sabbatical in 1963-64 and agreed to spend it in Salzburg, Austria, so I could go to the newly established Orff Institute. In line with his own interests, he arranged to work with Carl Orff on composition while I attended classes. Our youngest child, ten-year-old Anne, would accompany us and go to a local school. Elizabeth and John, our older children, were in college. We made arrangements to rent a small apartment in a "Schloss" in Aigen, just outside Salzburg, starting that fall.

I'll never forget the night we arrived in the rain and dark after a long drive from Amsterdam. We asked someone for directions and were told to "take the last bridge." Which one was that? Fortunately we guessed right and found our Schloss, a manor house that had been divided into apartments. We trod our way into the grandiose foyer in total darkness, found a light switch, and pushed it. Hunting trophies of deer, eagles, owls, and stags glared down at us from the walls! Then the light went out! We found the button again and quickly made our way up the long marble staircase to the second floor before we were again engulfed in the dark. When we reached the landlord's Wapartment on the top floor, a girl about Anne's age answered the door and called out "They're here!" before she ran back inside. And so we were.

We had reached Salzburg but the Orff Institute was far from ready for us. At the first meeting of the faculty and students in the dark and dismal basement of the Mozarteum, we were amazed to hear Dr. Orff and the faculty still discussing what they were going to do with us! We students were asked to play our recorders for the faculty. I remember performing a movement from a Telemann trio sonata and having Professor Tenta, the early music man, suggest a new trill fingering at the final cadence. We learned then that our classes would meet in the Mozarteum and in the basement of the Mirabell Palace until the Orff Institute's new building was finished in mid November. My daughter came into town for her weekly classes at the Mozarteum, and we always celebrated afterwards with a stop at a nearby Konditorei for a treat.

The first days were very full. I recall private harpsichord lessons with Frau Kupor and singing in the Mozarteum Choir. Our movement lessons with Barbara Haselbach were held in the large basement room of the Mirabell, where we had to dodge around the skinny pillars erratically scattered in the room. One of our classmates was Loris Tjeknavorian, a young Armenian composer who had come with the understanding that the Orff Institute was a school for composers. He was simply appalled at being expected to move, and faded into the woodwork as fast as possible. He dropped out of class but kept coming back at Orff's insistence again and again until he finally gave up and started working on his own. He eventually became the director of the national Armenian orchestra and a widely recognized composer. A good friend, he later came to the US to study.

The Orff Institute finally opened in mid-November with a series of ceremonial events. There were long lectures and addresses by important figures from Bavarian politics, education, and music. All, of course, in German. One evening, all of the students were summoned to an evening session at the new Institute. We found fourteen distinguished personages sitting at the entrance to a big movement room we'd never seen before, our faculty hovering around, and Dr. Orff in the middle of the room with a vast number of percussion instruments – most of which we'd never seen before, either – set up or lying on the floor in front of him. He invited us to come and claim an instrument.

Then he proceeded to conduct us in a magical percussion improvisation that made the most of every available timbre. After the applause, he turned to us and asked for a volunteer. Long pause. A student rose to the occasion, but she led us through an unimpressive exploration, whereupon Orff pounced on her mercilessly, criticizing everything she'd done. Then he asked for another volunteer. Long pause. He asked again. No response. Then he invited me to take a turn – twice – and twice I declined, much as I would have enjoyed the opportunity under other circumstances. But that was never to happen.

Orff was obviously not a born teacher. From our first encounter on, I saw that Gunild Keetman was. I was convinced then and there that the Orff movement would never have swept the world without Keetman's enormous contribution to the repertoire and her incomparable teaching skills. In later years we corresponded and exchanged photos and news. I sent her copies of my books and she sent me copies of hers. She also gave me two of her beautiful woven wall hangings, which I shall always treasure, along with a very good photo. It greets me every morning as I sit at my desk.

I remember so vividly the sessions we had with her at the Orff Institute, especially the hour and a half we spent one Wednesday morning on hand drum technique. She introduced us to the three basic techniques used in the Güntherschule days.

There was standing technique, holding the drum in the non-dominant hand and playing with the dominant thumb in the lower half of the drum head, with the fingers near the upper rim. Then finger technique, similar to standing technique but with the thumb and fingers playing near the middle of the drumhead, and smaller arm movements. Then ambidextrous technique, seated, with the drum held between the knees and both hands playing alternately, the thumb-strokes in the middle of the drumhead and the fingers at the rim. I've delighted in using these techniques ever since.

That first year the faculty seemed to be feeling its way. Most of the teaching was directed at developing our skills with little reference to the children we expected to teach. But I very much enjoyed Professor Keller's class in Theory and Composition, the first I'd taken since my graduate work at the University of Chicago. Still, it was far beyond most of the other students who were just out of teacher training courses and had minimal theory under their belts. So I did a good deal of coaching.

In that year at the Institute I also enjoyed my private lessons on harpsichord with Frau Kupor, the weekly playing sessions with my recorder teacher, Frau Tenta, and our two daily movement classes with Barbara Haselbach and Dagmar Bauz. In Lotte Flach's daily repertoire classes we played through a good part of Volumes I to V. We also observed the weekly children's class (in which our Anne participated) taught by Professor Keller and Dagmar Bauz. In the second term, Dr. Orff offered to give me private lessons in composition. He was at his best one on one, and could always put his finger on the spots that had caused me trouble in the pieces I brought to my lessons.

Too soon, our sabbatical year drew to a close. Our two older children joined us and the whole family went from Salzburg to a Catholic church music Workshop in Amiens, France, where my husband and I would be teaching. We were the only Americans and the only Protestants in a bevy of priests and nuns and Catholic musicians. Arriving early, we stopped along the roadside to practice a five-part madrigal we expected to sing later. As we stood along the country road, framed with trees along either side, we began to sing – just as a motorcyclist passed by. He stared at us incredulously.

From France we went traveling on to England and Wales. I left my husband and older children to explore my Hebridean heritage in Scotland. Anne and I had to head back to the US as I was to teach the Orff summer course at Ball State. I was now a graduate of the Orff Institute.

This essay was previously unpublished. It was written c. 1990.

4. AOSA Beginnings and The Orff Echo

After Salzburg, on my return to Indianapolis, I taught my first Orff workshop at Ball State (Muncie, Indiana) in the summer of 1964. Elizabeth Nichols, Sister Eloise McCormick, and Mimi Samuelson were there, among many others, and they became good friends and colleagues as the Orff movement developed in this country.

As with many foundational moments, several pieces have to fall into place before a new organization sees the light of day. It was not until after Martha Smith's stimulating 1967 Bellflower Symposium in California and Arnold Burkart's move to Ball State that the Midwestern Orff enthusiasts started to explore the possibility of forming a professional Orff organization. We met in each other's houses – at Arnold's in Muncie, at Ruth Hamm's in Cleveland, at Jake (Jacobeth) Postl's in Chicago, and at my home in Indianapolis.

This had its lighter moments as we went about stoking our mutual enthusiasm for the Orff Approach. I particularly remember a time when lanky and tall Joe Matthesius arrived at my doorstep, uncurling from his Volkswagen to his full height, ready for our meeting. On the wrong weekend!

There were a good many Orff colleagues within driving distance and we gradually worked out our plans. But when the OSA (Orff-Schulwerk Association) was officially organized by ten founders at Arnold's house on May 11, 1968, I was in Oxford, England, of all places. That's where my husband Jim's second sabbatical had taken us. (The organization was later renamed the American Orff-Schulwerk Association.)

Back in Indianapolis, I was ready for our first National Conference in 1969 in Muncie. I remember quite vividly the sessions by Jake Postl and Jacques Schneider, whose group of children performed almost too perfectly. My children's recorder class gave a demonstration, playing duets and trios and improvising. Additionally, our Carley family consort provided a concert, with recorders, viol, krummhorns, hand drum, and voices. Since we were lucky enough to have a soprano, alto, tenor, and baritone in the family, we could sing all the parts ourselves.

THE ORFF ECHO LAUNCHES

While we were still in England in 1968, I received a long letter from Elizabeth Nichols asking me to edit the new organization's newsletter. I agreed to a brief stint, only to find myself serving as the *Echo* editor for the next fifteen years.

Initially I was the entire editorial board. I wrote articles, book reviews, editorials, and requested or assigned articles to others. Then I sent everything to the printer, corrected the proofs, pasted up the paper, got it printed, and mailed it out to our members. It proved to be a bigger job than I anticipated, not made any easier by contributors' manuscripts that had a habit of arriving somewhat later than requested.

The first issue of *The Orff Echo* appeared in November 1968. It was four pages long and included a greeting from Carl Orff (*auf Deutsch*), a message from our first president, Arnold Burkart, a letter from Salzburg from Joe Matthesius, an article by Margaret Murray, reports from Memphis and Chicago, "Names in the News," "Suggestions for Christmas Repertoire" from the Schulwerk, a letter to members requesting more articles and news, and a short Membership Analysis claiming a total of about 160 souls in the Association.

The newsletter had to be planned months in advance, and every issue took weeks of work. There were no ads at all from the music industry until 1975, when suddenly seven launched in the September issue. I was always trying to get ahead of the game with assignments for future issues. An expanded editorial board eventually developed, with regular meetings. As the *Echo* grew into a magazine, we set the focus for each issue, chose what books to review, and determined the articles to assign.

Six years in, and after my husband retired, we moved to Brasstown, North Carolina in 1974. The work became more time-consuming. The printer was some distance away and everything was done by mail. By this time there was an advisory board, which met three times a year, usually in Chicago in connection with the AOSA Board meetings. My working hours were yet to diminish.

I had to send everything except my editorials and the book reviews to all the board members and wait for their responses before I could forward anything to the printer. So I found myself always working two or three issues ahead, assigning articles well before I could publish them. In later years a volunteer put together a big four-page centerfold for each issue. I particularly remember those by Judy Thomas, Esther Gray, and Tossi Aaron. Somewhere along the line I was awarded a yearly stipend of $500. That helped, too.

My final issue as Editor of *The Orff Echo* went out in the summer of 1983. It was a twenty-four page, professional magazine, with seven articles, a four-page centerfold – this one by Gin Ebinger – a long editorial, six short news reports, columns by Elizabeth Nichols and Tossi Aaron, and five book reviews. The editorial board then consisted of Maydelle Meier (Advertising Manager), Tossi Aaron, Pat Brown, Gin Ebinger, Esther Gray, Beth Miller, Elizabeth Nichols, Jacobeth Postl, and me.

It was a pleasure to see how the *Echo* had grown. It reflected well on the AOSA and served our membership with distinction.

(*Orff Re-Echoes*, Books I and II, contain many of the best articles from my years as Editor.)

This essay was previously unpublished.

5. Gunild Keetman, In Appreciation

Gunild Keetman's role in the development of the Orff ensemble and the Schulwerk can never be exaggerated. She was the first to experiment with the original box-xylophone, brought by chance to the Güntherschule by a sailor. As a director of the famous Güntherschule Ensemble of young adult dancers and musicians, Keetman put together, one instrument at a time, the original ensemble of pitched and unpitched percussion instruments, recorders, strings, and bar instruments. It was she who composed the music for their performances – long before there was any inkling of the role the ensemble would play in the music education of children.

She also wrote most of the early Orff Schulwerk repertoire during the Güntherschule days and all the delightful "little gray books" used to this day by Orff teachers. When the Orff Ensemble was revived in 1948, Keetman adjusted the repertoire to the level of the eight to twelve-year-olds in her demonstration group. She wrote or arranged the music for the pioneering radio programs broadcast to schools in Bavaria and taught the children who participated. The "Orff Schulwerk" for children was born.

As far as I know, Orff himself never taught children. Certainly he didn't the year I was at the Orff Institute.

For the 1949 radio programs, the emphasis had to be on speech play, simple songs (traditional or newly composed), and simple accompaniments. There was obviously no way to demonstrate movement training. The supporting ensemble included body percussion, a great variety of unpitched percussion instruments, and what remained of the bar instruments from the Güntherschule days. Almost all instruments, costumes, photographs, the library, and archives had been destroyed in World War II.

As is well known, the response to the programs was so widespread and so enthusiastic that the radio series went on for years. This led eventually to the development of the new Orff-Schulwerk edition for children published by Schott Music, as well as many supplementary instruction books issued for years afterwards.

THE LEGACY OF GUNILD KEETMAN'S WORKS

The little gray books by Gunild Keetman are unfortunately very little known on this side of the Atlantic. Published by Schott from 1951 to 1973, many of them are from the Güntherschule days and, unfortunately, are too demanding to be used in the short training courses typically held in the United States and Canada.

Let me mention a few of my favorites:

- *Stücke für Blockflöten I-a* and *I-b*, 1951
- *Stücke für Blockflöten und Kleines Schlagwerk*, 1952
- *Stücke für Flöte und Trommel I*, 1956
- *Lieder für die Schule III*, 1961; *IV*, 1963; *V*, 1963; *VI*, 1965; *VII*, 1967
- *Spielbuch für Xylophon I*, 1965
- *Spielbuch für Xylophon II*, 1966
- *Erstes Spiel am Xylophon*, 1969
- *Stücke für Flöte und Trommel II*, 1973

Gunild Keetman's incomparable *Elementaria, First Acquaintance with Orff-Schulwerk*, (published in English in 1974) is likewise neglected in North America. Add to this her delightful Christmas carol settings in *Singen und Spielen zu Weihnachten* by Gunild Keetman and Minne Ronnefeld – doubtless because so few are in English.

It is common knowledge that almost all of the instrumental pieces in the five volumes of the Schulwerk in German and English are by Keetman, while most of the song settings are by Orff. I find her settings far more varied and inventive than many of Orff's arrangements. In Volume I, for instance, there are several delightful little instrumental pieces by her in *La* Pentatonic, and many others with accompanying ostinati shifting back and forth between *Do* and *La* Pentatonic that provide a delightful tension underlying the melodies themselves. (See p. 104ff.)

Since the repertoire in the five volumes of the Schulwerk is far better known than the contents of her supplementary books, I want to concentrate on two unfamiliar books of Keetman's which I consider the most immediately useful.

Erstes Spiel am Xylophon limits its repertoire to the pentatonic scale (C D E G A C), but *any* tone may be the tonal center. The tunes are not limited to C Pentatonic, as in most instruction books. Initially, the child plays the accompaniment as the teacher sings. Before long, many of the children can both sing and play. Additional accompanying patterns are suggested for the first few *So-Mi* songs to traditional rhymes, so that each child is immediately challenged at his or her own level. The first accompanying patterns are octaves or fifths on the beat: C and C' or C and G. Then "ta-ti taa" patterns on the same notes are suggested.

Already on the second *So-Mi* song, the supplementary accompaniments introduce half the third song – still on *So* and *Mi* – using two consecutive patterns: octave quarter notes as the introduction and alternating C'-G-C'-A quarter notes to support the melody.

In #4 the vocal range is extended to *So-Mi-La* and there are two sets of four different accompanying patterns, plus four suggested alternatives! Every child is being challenged at his or her own level. Where else have you ever seen such a choice at so early a stage? In #7 the accompanying pattern requires repeated eighth notes. The accompaniment for #8 requires alternating quarter notes on C octaves in the A section; alternating E octaves in the B section; and alternating G octaves in the C section, where the initial tune is stretched to cover over an octave (C D E G A C' D' E'). The melody requires the new technique of alternating hands on a scale pattern: L-R-L-R on C D E G throughout the A and C sections; R-L-R-L in the B section on E' D' C' A as the melody descends. The following piece is a variation on #8, now in triple meter, with a descending scale as the ostinato accompaniment in A and C alternates G A G and A G A patterns in the B section.

Further Keetman pieces introduce a great variety of new ostinato patterns, some covering a surprisingly wide range on the accompanying xylophone as well as rhythmic variations of the melodies, like in #16 where dotted eighths and sixteenths are introduced. Six-eight meter appears first in #23 as a variation of #22. In #31, the melody involves both rapid eighth note scale patterns and a double-patterned accompaniment with alternating thirds and fourths in the right hand on C' and E', D' and G', C' and E' again, and A and D' over repeated eighth notes on middle C in the left hand. Scalewise patterns occur in #35 in triple meter on G A C' D' E' G' to support a descending melody. Patterns in contrary motion appear in #42, both in the melody and in its accompaniment, and the book ends with a set of little canons for two players or two groups.

It seems to me that this book alone provides a wonderfully stimulating example of what we teachers can do with the simplest materials from our own traditions. We can tailor the accompaniments to the skill of each student and, in turn, add or subtract parts as needed. We can work out appropriate movement games or body percussion to enrich these basic musical experiences for the young children we teach.

The repertoire in *Spielbuch fur Xylophon I*, Keetman's second book for xylophone published in 1969, was actually written much earlier for the Güntherschule students. Already it is limited to the pentatonic realm, but, impressively, not only to the familiar *Do* Pentatonic scale. In the introduction, Keetman calls attention to the possibility of using any of the five tones as the final. The first little piece, for example, is in *La* Pentatonic, with the right hand playing a complete phrase *forte* and the left hand answering *piano*. At the end, the right hand plays G and A half notes, the left hand echoes, and the pattern is repeated before the initial phrase is played by the right hand.

Pieces #3-6 are all in *La* Pentatonic, while #7, #12, and #13 are all in *Re* Pentatonic. *So* tunes also appear. Those labeled *Mi* Pentatonic are less convincing. But I find it truly astonishing that Gunild Keetman, growing up in Germany where there is no tradition of pentatonic song whatever, discovered for herself the possibilities of using any tone of the pentatonic scale as the final, as frequently occurs in so many Scottish, Irish, and American folk songs.

The F Pentatonic scale is introduced in #21 and #22, and its relative minor on D in #24. There are also some convincing minor pentatonic tunes on E in #26, #27, #29 and #30. Then comes a surprising series of pentatonic tunes with half steps, on E F G B C; on E F A B D'; on G B C' D' F' before we reach the last section of the book, in which pentatonic tunes in *La* Pentatonic, *So* Pentatonic, *Re* Pentatonic and *Mi* Pentatonic are to be sung over their increasingly demanding xylophone accompaniments. Presumably the singer both plays and sings – rather a daunting assignment.

The other little gray books I've most enjoyed are those for recorders: *Spielstücke für Blockflöten 1A* and *Spielstücke für Blockflöten IB*, dated 1932; and my favorite, *Pieces for Hand Drums and Recorders* (1956). *Spielstücke fur Blockflöten und Kleines Schlagwerk* is dated 1930 – obviously composed for the Güntherschule ensemble – but not published until 1952. It is, needless to say, far beyond grade school children, but not their teachers.

Keetman's *Elementaria: First Acquaintance with Orff-Schulwerk* was first published in Germany in 1970, and in an English translation by Margaret Murray in 1974. It is an invaluable guide to aspiring and experienced Orff teachers alike, spelling out concisely and clearly the ideal sequence and content of beginning lessons. Unlike other such books, it's impressively succinct.

Keetman suggests many ways of developing a piece:
- Repeating it an octave higher.
- Changing the dynamics.
- Alternating solo and tutti.
- Changing instrumental groups.
- Changing the meter.
- Adding body percussion, unpitched percussion, introduction, interludes, coda.
- Using it for movement accompaniment.

Part I of *Elementaria* ends with many examples of speech exercises accompanied by body percussion – weather rhymes, names of trees and flowers, and a few proverbs and traditional sayings. Any of them would provide a good basis for improvisation and/or composition.

Part II is concerned with Elementary Movement Training and remains the only adequate guide to musical movement training in relation to the Orff Approach that I have ever seen. How I wish it had been in print when I started teaching Orff to both children and adults!

After quoting Orff's famous statement, "Elemental music is never music alone, but forms a unity with movement, dance, and speech," Keetman adds: "This unity that even today is quite natural to many cultures and needs no special fostering has in most civilized lands been entirely lost, and carried on in an unbroken line only by children. To preserve and develop this unity for children is one of the main tasks that Orff Schulwerk has set itself. It requires, besides the development of musical and language abilities, an elementary movement training … able to provide, through the strong emphasis on rhythmical elements, a reciprocal benefit to musical skills." And she adds, "In principal, no Schulwerk lesson should be without movement activities."

Short segments on Movement Pieces, Elementary Movement Improvisation, and Movement Accompaniment are impressive. Let me quote Keetman: "The aim and purpose of movement accompaniment is both to support and to stimulate the movement, whether through rhythm, melody, or both. The main criterion is that the accompaniment must be appropriate for the movement, whether it consists of clapping, finger-snapping, speech, humming or singing, or performed upon an instrument." And again: "An accompaniment that remains always at the same level of intensity has a deadening effect, but one that is varied and keeps returning to very soft playing stimulates attention. Complete cessation of the accompaniment here and there increases its attractiveness when it recurs."

Later, she adds: "The aim of melodic movement accompaniment for children is to prepare them for later improvisation, whether on bar instruments or recorders. To avoid the danger of monotony the ostinato should be changed frequently. For long improvisations, two or more predetermined ostinati can be used alternately."

A page and a half of invaluable "Suggestions for movement lessons for beginners" (*i.e.*, children from four to six) and another page and a half of "Further suggestions for the slightly more experienced" conclude the main text. In an Appendix there are guidelines and photos that show the playing of the supplementary percussion instruments, plus fine photos of the entire Orff Ensemble. There is an extensive list of publications from the Orff Institute and from Schott, including all of Gunild Keetman's little gray books and her *Christmas Story* with a text by Orff.

In only one way can I sum up all this extended discussion that is so necessary to see the scope and breadth of her work. I know of no other book that provides such expert guidance for teachers in all aspects of the Orff Approach as her *Elementaria*. Simply, it is a pedagogical masterpiece. And Keetman has left us all a priceless legacy.

This essay was previously unpublished. It was written in 1991.

6. The Magic Carpet of Sound

The most characteristic and delightful stage in the Orff Approach has always seemed to me to be use of the Drone-Ostinato style, with its opportunities for both extreme simplicity and surprising sophistication. Its basic elements of drone and short melodic ostinato, provide the simplest means of making ensemble music – and the most universal. Yet the skillful layering and overlapping of these independent patterns weaves a fabric of increasing vitality and complexity as the patterns respond to each other and to the melody they accompany. Although the actual notes and patterns remain the same, their musical meaning changes. As more parts are introduced, the relationships between the individual patterns, and between the combined patterns and the overlying melody, affect the meaning of the entire piece.

The Drone-Ostinato style reaches its apex in these increasingly complex relationships. Overarching free melodies follow their own necessary course above the entire ensemble, rolling out the carpet of sound, as Orff termed it. The drone is the floor on which everything rests; the carpet is all the interlocking repetitive patterns of contrasting shapes and colors woven in sound. It fills the room, pulsing with life as our ear learns to perceive the skillfully wrought relationships we had missed on first hearing – the astonishing rhythmic polyphony between the separate patterns, the skillful accommodation of whatever harmonic implications may lurk in the melodies, and the amazing use of dissonance as the texture thickens and the patterns multiply.

At the start the supporting drone is as simple as can be, and as natural. It is only the bilateral playing of open fifths on the pulse to support a two- or three-tone melody, with no contrasting ostinato at all. The carpet at this point seems monochromatic, but the rhythm is continuous, neatly camouflaging the phrase-breaks in the tune. Soon, however, the texture will thicken, with a third part added on a contrasting instrument, and away we go. We are off on a long and rewarding journey through pentatonic, hexatonic, and diatonic modes, with increasingly complex interrelated patterns providing tonal and rhythmic support for increasingly complex melodies.

It seems to me that Orff's carpet of sound is a wonderful image to keep in mind. When choosing, arranging, or composing repertoire in this style, it keeps us focused on the underlying rhythmic continuity within a section in a long piece, or right to the end of a short one. Orff's carpet unfolds whole. The patterns are not interrupted again and again, but continue quite independently of the phrase breaks in the melody itself. There are no holes in the carpet of sound! The patterns provide a forward impetus at every phrase break in the melody as the rhythm continues its hypnotic movement into the next phrase, and the next.

This is how rhythmic security is built in the Orff Approach. Repetitive large-muscle movement, with its congenial relaxing power, will be expressed in locomotor movement, body percussion exercises, or the playing of unpitched percussion and the bar instruments. A common pulse becomes internalized, so that ensemble playing becomes possible. Orff was wise enough to know all this long before developmental psychologists told us so, and then used it as a basis for a new approach to music education.

Yet it seems to me that Orff's style offers far more than this. Perhaps the image of his colorful carpet of sound is too static to give an accurate impression of the amazing alchemy he has wrought with such simple means. The image should be dynamic, like this cosmos we inhabit, full of independent entities going their separate ways. Sometimes they are colliding, sometimes adjusting to each other, sometimes fusing and moving on together, sometimes growing and changing their relationships.

Physicists and mystics tell us the same thing, that reality consists of waves of light and sound in everlasting motion. The old notion of the "music of the spheres" is alive again in our day. Do we not hear for ourselves the humming of Saturn's rings? The old duality of living things and dead matter is gone for good. The dance of life – the dance of Shiva in Hindu philosophy – gives us a more apt image to encompass the living, pulsing, immediacy of Orff's idiomatic style. For his notes are the atoms of physics; his ostinati are small entities in endless patterned movement; his melodies, complex living creatures of our human imagination, each with its own character and destiny. The simple "elemental" style Orff developed is proving far more elemental than he dreamed!

A version of this essay first appeared in The Orff Echo Volume 24 Issue 4 [Summer 1992]. Reprinted with permission from The Orff Echo, the quarterly journal published by the American Orff-Schulwerk Association.

7. The Musical Realm of the Pentatonic

When I studied music theory there was no mention of any kind of pentatonic scale and only passing mention of the diatonic modes into which some theorists claim they evolved – Ionian, Dorian, Phrygian, Mixolydian, and Aeolian – and with which we concern ourselves in the Orff Approach. Any development of pentatonic theory has therefore been a gradual accretion of experience in using pentatonic scales in teaching, in improvisation, in composition, and in collecting and analyzing a great number of pentatonic folk tunes, mainly from our North American heritage.

What got me started thinking beyond the obvious use of *Do* Pentatonic in Volume I was a conversation I had with Dr. Richard Johnston of the University of Toronto. He was visiting in Salzburg during the year I spent at the Orff Institute. He quoted Daniel Hellden as saying that there was more to the pentatonic than the "gapped major" scale used in Volume I. That was all, but it stuck in my mind, and as I began to hunt for pentatonic songs from our own tradition, I became more and more aware that many of them were indeed anchored on tones other than *Do*.

I kept hunting and collecting examples of the less likely pentatonic modes, finding many examples of *La* Pentatonic; a few *Re* and *So* Pentatonics, especially among songs from the southern mountains; and not a single *Mi* Pentatonic to date, although many of the three- or four-tone playground chants seem to be centered on *Mi*, at least when they are allowed to stand alone without accompaniment.

PENTATONIC THEORY

As Professor Keller pointed out at the St. Louis Orff AOSA Conference (1978), there are not only the authentic modes to be considered, but also their plagal variants, so that with only the tones of any *Do* Pentatonic scale we have at our disposal ten different modes! For example, if we use only the tones of the C Pentatonic scale, we have the following possibilities:

Authentic	*Plagal*
Do Pentatonic	
C D E G A C'	G A **C'** D' E' G'
Re Pentatonic	
D E G A C' D'	A C **D'** E' G' A'
Mi Pentatonic	
E G A C' D' E'	A C' D' **E'** G' A'
So Pentatonic	
G A C' D' E' G'	D E **G** A C' D'
La Pentatonic	
A C' D' E' G' A'	E G **A** C' D' E'

Of course, some tunes extend beyond the range of an octave, but the point is that the shape and character of any melody is partly dependent on the position of the final in the tune. Does it lie at the top or bottom, as in the authentic modes, or in the middle, as in the plagal modes?

Tunes in *La* or *So* Pentatonic modes in the C Pentatonic setup are likely to be plagal, since the final lies in the middle of the vocal range. Those in *Do* or *Re* Pentatonic are likely to be authentic, with the final near the bottom of the vocal range. In F and G Pentatonic setups, the reverse is true: tunes in *Do* or *Re* Pentatonic modes are likely to be plagal and those in *So* and *La* are likely to be authentic.

Instrumental pieces, of course, are far freer to use either form of the mode, whatever the scale setup, since they are not restricted to the vocal range. In any case, *any* tone of the pentatonic scale may be the tonal center (for which the pentatonic mode is named) and *any* pentatonic mode may be either authentic or plagal.

On the diatonic bar instruments, then, we have the possibility of using the complete set of pentatonic modes in C Pentatonic, F Pentatonic, G Pentatonic, B♭ Pentatonic, and D Pentatonic. Fifty possible scales just in the limited range of the diatonic instruments! With such riches at our disposal it behooves us to explore the possibilities of the pentatonic in far greater depth than has been customary, both in studying our heritage of folk songs and in improvisation, arranging, and composition.

The following chart may make more immediately visible the authentic modes of the C Pentatonic scale:

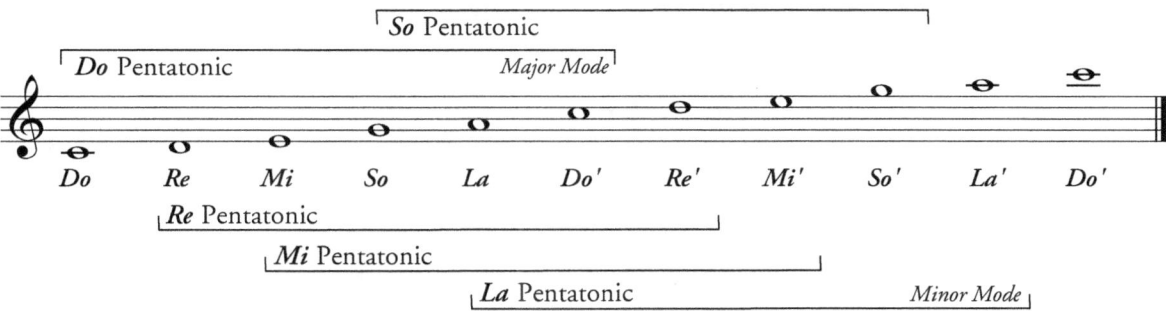

The chart makes clear that the spacing of the intervals varies from mode to mode: *Do* Pentatonic lacks the fourth and seventh degrees; *Re* lacks the third and the sixth; *Mi* omits both the second and the fifth; *So* has neither third nor seventh; *La* lacks both the second and the sixth. With these gaps in different positions within the octave, melodies in the various modes sound very different, one from another. Indeed, some pentatonic tunes defy ready analysis and seem quite ambiguous, so that assigning them to one mode or another seems arbitrary. Since these songs were never accompanied, this ambiguity bothered no one, and may have added a welcome element of unpredictability. (The shape of the tunes varies too, depending on where the final lies.)

PENTATONIC FOLK SONGS

One very good reason for us to take seriously the pentatonic modes we've been discussing is that we have in this country an incomparably rich heritage of pentatonic folk songs. We, as music teachers, need to know them and pass them on to the children we teach. Among these traditional songs are children's songs, play-party songs, ballads, love songs, folk hymns and carols – an astonishing wealth of beautiful and memorable songs of rare aesthetic value. Such songs (like **Black, Black, Black**; **Poor Wayfaring Stranger**;

Resignation; **Barbara Ellen**; **A la Claire Fontaine**; **The Riddle Song**; **Wondrous Love**; **Nottamun Town**) are among the loveliest in the English language, treasures far beyond the kindergarten and primary children for whom the pentatonic realm is usually reserved. Let us not neglect these songs and their equals in our hurry to reach more familiar harmonic ground.

Before the full pentatonic scale is introduced, two-tone, three-tone, and four-tone chants and tunes should be found or improvised. Theorists differ as to how to refer to them – whether as partial pentatonics, or as things in themselves. Many of these limited range songs are tonally ambiguous, since they require no accompaniment whatsoever in their playground incarnations and imply no harmonic center. The choice of a supporting bordun may not be obvious, and may indeed be somewhat arbitrary.

When, for example, there are only three tones, A, G and E, in a tune, it may sound quite convincing with a C - G bordun, like ⓐ in which all the accents fall on either *So* or *Mi*:

If, however, the same tune is used but the rhythm changed so that it starts with an upbeat, as in ⓑ, it sounds better with an A - E bordun:

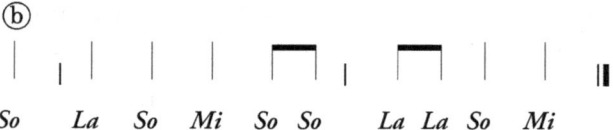

Other three- and four-tone songs may feel clearly minor, like ⓒ, **Hammer Ring**:

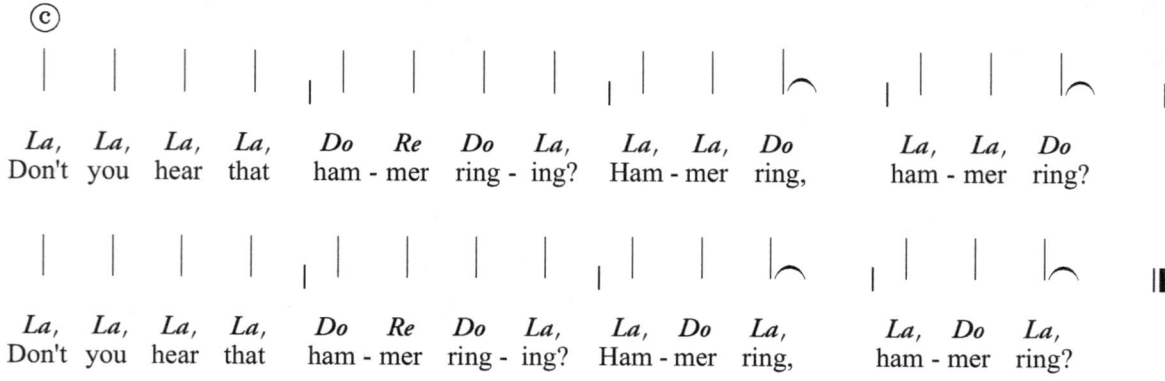

or ⓓ, **Mary Mack**, with its delightful opportunity for shifting accompaniment using both the tonic and the submediant fifths or chords:

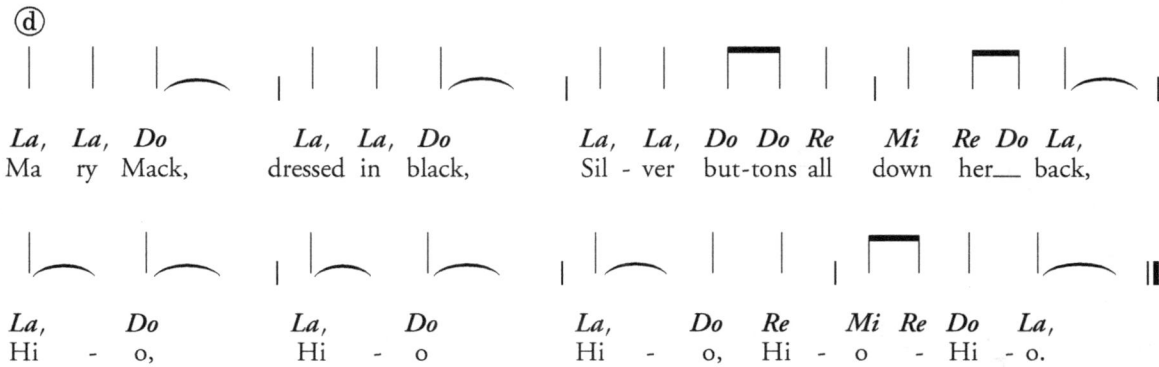

There are, of course, innumerable songs in *Do* Pentatonic, both authentic and plagal, in our tradition. Let me remind you of a few, without taking the space to quote them. Among the authentic tunes are **The Barnyard Song**, **Kansas Boys**, **Tideo**, **Jim Along, Josie**, **Willowbee**, and **Restless Sea**, with its pleasing play between major and minor. Familiar plagal songs are **Cotton-Eye Joe**, **Toodala**, **All Night, All Day**, **Angel Band**, **Night Herding Song**, and Abraham Lincoln's favorite, **Hoosen Johnny**.

La Pentatonic tunes may not be quite so familiar. I'll mention a few (all authentic): **Land of the Silver Birch**, **Dear Companion**, **My Good Old Man**, Richard Chase's version of **Cock Robin**, **Wayfaring Stranger**, **Edward**, and that marvelously surreal song, **Nottamun Town**.

Plagal examples are **Down in the Meadow**, **The Birds' Courting Song**, **Stewball**, a great favorite, and **The Cherry Tree Carol** from Western North Carolina:

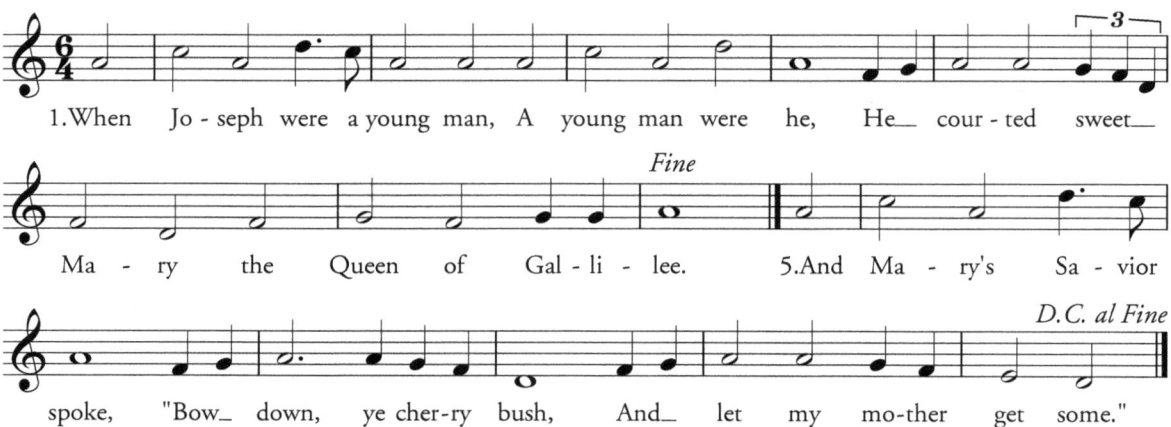

Clay County, North Carolina

Pentatonic modes without the third – *Re* and *So* – sound strange and mysterious to our ears. It takes time and practice to feel comfortable with them, either in singing folk songs or in improvising. The *Re* mode, for instance, has the new possibility of using the low seventh, particularly in cadences, and its major triad as a melodic motive. You'll hear this in the following examples:

ⓐ **Shady Grove**

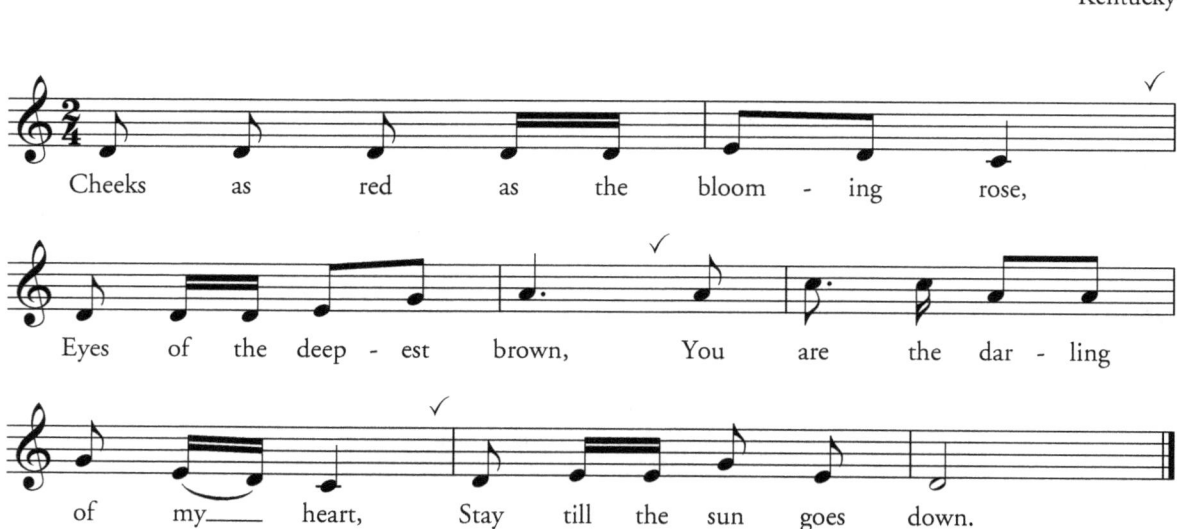

Kentucky

ⓑ **Daily Growing**   (*Re* Pentatonic, Plagal)

So Pentatonic, on the other hand, requires unusual melodic emphasis on its dominant to be convincingly anchored on *So*, and may also involve frequent use of the second degree, *La*, and its minor triad. Without this emphasis on *Re*, the tune may sound more like *Do* plagal than *So*. The well-known **Riddle Song**, which seems to shift from *Do* plagal to *So* and back again, so that either drone sounds questionable, is usually classified as *So* Pentatonic. Here are two clearer examples of *So* Pentatonic tunes, one of the many variants of **Lord Thomas and Fair Elinor** in the Cecil Sharp collection and **Pretty Saro**:

Lord Thomas and Fair Elinor   (*So* Pentatonic, Authentic)

Pretty Saro (*So* Pentatonic, Authentic)

Southern Appalachians

1. Down in some lone val - ley, In a lone - some place, Where the wild birds do whist - le, and their notes do in -crease, Fare -well pret -ty_ Sa - ro, I bid you a - dieu, But I'll dream of pret -ty Sa - ro wher - e - ver I go.
2. My love she won't have me, So I un - der -stand, She_ wants a free - hol -der who_ owns house and land. I can -not main -tain her with sil - ver and gold, Nor buy all the_ fine things that a big house can hold.

Mi Pentatonic is a law unto itself, with its third but no fifth, and requires more emphasis on the tonic than any of the other pentatonic modes to make it convincing. It is usually reinforced with a tonic drone. As in its diatonic equivalent, the Phrygian mode, the fourth degree serves as the dominant in both authentic modes and the sixth in both plagal modes.

For example:

IMC

Most pentatonic songs are clearly anchored in one mode or another, though a few are tonally ambiguous and require patient analysis and experimentation before class use. It is sometimes possible, for instance, to mistake a *So* plagal tune for a *Re* authentic, and the only way to be sure is to analyze the tune itself to see whether the fourth or the fifth is used more frequently and more conspicuously. If the fourth is emphasized more, then chances are the tune's in *So* plagal and will sound best with a *So-Re* bordun. But if the fifth is more prominent, the tune lies in *Re* Pentatonic, and will sound best with a *Re-La* bordun.

A further caution: Some pentatonic tunes are indeed what Hellden called them – "gapped major" scale tunes. These are quite inappropriate for use in Orff-style arrangements because the harmonic implications are simply too strong to be ignored. Too much melodic emphasis on either the dominant or the second degree of the scale (particularly on accents or in cadences), or sustained notes on either interval, are clues to such tunes. Though one can, with ingenuity, invent ostinato patterns that accommodate occasional harmonic pulls, it is wiser to avoid such tunes altogether until we reach the harmonic stage and need not attempt to camouflage their basic harmonic nature.

PENTATONIC IMPROVISATION

It is not only for the sake of these wonderful old folk tunes that a study of pentatonic modes is valuable, rich as that tradition is. In my experience the use of all these pentatonic modes in improvisation from an early stage develops a real sensitivity to melodic structure and flavor that can be cultivated in no other way. There are *only* melodic concerns at this stage, with no harmonic implications or conventions to be accommodated. It is through improvisation that the character and melodic possibilities of each pentatonic mode become familiar, and the flavor of each can best be savored.

Before any group or solo assignments in improvisation can be successful, the intended pentatonic mode must be thoroughly established. If, for example the lesson is in *Re* Pentatonic, take the time to sing a familiar *Re* Pentatonic song like **Shady Grove** or **Betty Larkin** before launching into any preparatory drill.

One of the best ways to begin is with vocal group improvisation, following and mirroring the teacher's hand signs in simple, slow-moving melodic exercises, until the intervals and gestures are secure. Then a carefully built-up supporting ensemble may be added to reinforce the unfamiliar tonal center. It will be as simple or complex a carpet of sound as the particular group spontaneously invents. The teacher's guidance and aesthetic input from the class are key.

When they are ready to volunteer, students take turns assuming the teacher's role and lead the class in a melody of their own devising. Some memorable and magical improvisations have rewarded such ventures again and again. Echo play on scale figures, the full scale, and characteristic melodic motives prepare the way for Question+Answer play. Class rondos can combine set rondo themes, drawn from the Q+A improvisation, with spontaneous improvised interludes, the setting of a chosen poem, or the arrangement of a favorite folk song – whichever the class is ready to tackle.

Whatever the particular assignment, be sure to add at least one accompanying pattern yourself to lull your students into a comfortable right-brain state of mind, allowing their natural musicality free play. Then, even if somebody flubs, the music goes on, and there's a minimum of self-consciousness – particularly if you've made clear that everyone has good and bad days in improvising. Occasional disappointment is to be expected. No matter what the accompanying instrument, the results will be much better musically and much less threatening to the students than if the improvisation is unsupported. The physical movement involved in playing the accompanying patterns on the bar instruments, and the magical sounds they make, combine to produce an enveloping hypnotic effect that seems to disengage our critical, left-brain faculties and allows natural musicality to assert itself.

Let me add parenthetically that hand-sign improvisation is just as effective with instruments as with voices. I find that recorder players play much better in tune when they are following and thinking the precise tonal relationships the syllables invoke than when they are either reading or improvising without them. And certainly it's very easy to teach a phrase or an ostinato to a player in the ensemble who can sing the part correctly before trying to find it on an instrument.

Another advantage of using the pentatonic modes extensively in improvisation is that our students are unaware of the vast number of pentatonic songs they already know. Most students have never given a moment's thought to analyzing them because these tunes have usually been given unbecoming harmonic accompaniments. Their melodic character is obscured. As a result, when students have to improvise their own tunes and we choose to explore the pentatonic modes, they cannot simply reproduce tiresome, banal imitations of obvious melodic material, running blithely up to the dominant and back downstairs to the tonic. That seems invariably to happen when the transition to diatonic scales is made if melodic sensitivity has not been developed through improvisation.

Pentatonic improvisation can keep us all busy exploring far beyond the beginning stage. With such enormous resources at our fingertips, it should be obvious that we need never put the pentatonic realm behind us. We should not relegate it only to the initial stage of Orff training, but come back to it periodically to enrich our whole musical curriculum,

THE TRANSITION TO DIATONIC MODES

There is another very cogent reason, it seems to me, to take pentatonic theory seriously and to emphasize the use of the pentatonic modes both in our choice of song repertoire and in improvisation lessons. The use of pentatonic songs weans our students away from *Do* as the inevitable tonal center, so that the transition to the diatonic modes becomes an easy and natural progression – just the way the transition from *Do* Pentatonic to the hexatonic and full major scale has always been in the Orff Approach. When we are ready to move on to the diatonic modes, we need only fill in the holes in the familiar pentatonic modes: *Re* Pentatonic becomes the Dorian mode; *Mi* Pentatonic becomes the Phrygian; *So* Pentatonic becomes the Mixolydian; *La* Pentatonic becomes the Aeolian; and, of course, *Do* Pentatonic becomes the Ionian mode, our major scale. Only the Lydian (on the fourth degree) and the Locrian (on the seventh degree) remain to be introduced, and they are of little practical use with their inescapable diminished fifths.

Without this bridge, the move from pentatonic to diatonic scales often proves traumatic and astonishingly difficult, even for graduate students in Orff Certification courses. Indeed, this seems the most difficult stage in the Orff sequence for our students, to combine the familiar bordun-ostinato style of accompaniment from the pentatonic stage with the diatonic tunes of the modal stage without falling into the dominant and subdominant patterns that properly apply only to the next stage of functional harmony.

Conventional major and minor scales and tunes are comfortably familiar to our students at any age, whether preschool children or graduate students. It seems all too easy to jump prematurely into this familiar territory and to spend far too much time in its cozy confines. While undoubtedly a necessary stage in our students' musical education so that they become adept at using the time-honored functional harmony of our Western tradition, it's not sufficient. Now, at the end of the Twentieth Century, we are doing our students a serious disservice if we lock them into the outmoded conventions of the last two centuries, conventions that serious composers have discarded long since.

One of the great virtues of the Orff Approach seems to me to be its universality that frees it from the conventions of the Central European musical tradition of its birth. It can lead anywhere, musically speaking, anywhere our own interests lead. That can bring us to the enjoyment and performance of pop music, of our folk musics, of early music, of traditional symphonic repertoire, of music from other traditions, or of the most sophisticated contemporary styles.

CONCLUSION

Recurrent, thorough, and patient exploration of the pentatonic modes – in our heritage of folk song and in improvisation – multiplies tenfold the musical resources open to our students and us. Our students will learn what Orff intended, to play with the materials of music as a composer does.

A version of this essay first appeared in The Orff Echo Volume 15 Issue 4 [Summer 1983]. Reprinted with permission from The Orff Echo, the quarterly journal published by the American Orff-Schulwerk Association.

Part Two

Practicum

Where do we begin? We begin where the children are. Make use of their fascination with language by exploring the possibilities of speech play; make use of their natural impulse toward movement by exploring their own natural movement before trying to impose an external beat; make use of their delight in rhythmic play with the body rhythms that Orff so skillfully developed into a musical vocabulary.

    IMC in "Where Then Do We Begin?"

8. Where Then Do We Begin?

One need only look at the very first page of the first volume of *Music for Children* to be aware of the need for pre-Orff training. The demands are already quite sophisticated. Consider, for example, the first song, **Cuckoo,** where the children are expected to be able to (1) sing on pitch this simple two-tone tune and (2) accompany their singing with a series of astonishingly demanding rhythm patterns, not a single one of which simply reinforces the pulse. That usual first rhythmic demand that we make of beginners is not found here. And then they are being asked to shift patterns in the middle of this very short song!

Turn the page, and what do we find? **Tinker Tailor**, another *So-Mi* tune with challenging alternative accompaniments. One requires independent movement of the two hands (sometimes parallel, sometimes contrary) and at the bottom of the page, rapid alternating octaves on an alto glockenspiel! Two pages later, **Little Tommy Tucker** provides three contrasting ostinati in each of the accompanying parts in the space of ten measures. Then the last section has triplets in the melody against two eighths in the glockenspiel part, over a steady *pizzicato* bordun in the bass.

When we move on to **Unk, Unk, Unk**, a multitude of new techniques are needed: four mallets on alto xylophone. Moving borduns, paraphony, syncopations. A third ostinato for alto xylophone in the final section, requiring alternately three and two mallets. Solo and tutti singing in a full octave range. And so it goes. There *are* some much easier settings interspersed between these difficult ones, such as **Bobby Shaftoe**, **The Baker**, and the popular canons **Diggidiggidong** and **Ding Dong, The Bells Do Ring**.

The same holds true when we proceed to the speech and rhythm exercises in Volume I, Part II. They are not as easy as they seem, and the progression is astonishingly rapid. The insertion of many other original exercises to bridge the sudden skips appears to be a necessity. Similarly, the instrumental pieces in Part III take for granted the children's ability to stay together, to play parallel octaves and moving borduns, *etc*. One has to know the Orff-Schulwerk repertoire thoroughly to find a workable progression from one relatively "easy" piece to another.

My review of these first songs and instrumental pieces in Volume I makes clear that the following skills were assumed:

1. The students can maintain a common pulse.
2. They can hear more than their own parts and can sing one part while playing another, or move to music their classmates are playing.
3. They can hold onto an independent part against other independent parts. That is, playing quarter-note against two eighth-notes, quarter-note against half-note, or whatever rhythmic combination is required.
4. They can hear the form of the piece they are performing, instantly adjusting to new accompanying ostinato patterns at each new section.
5. They can play with considerable technique involving (a) independent movement of the two hands, (b) rapid cross-over patterns, (c) scale patterns, (d) parallel octaves, (e) use of multiple mallets, (f) accurate playing of off-beats and syncopations, (g) use of glissandi, and (h) rapid changes in technique from one section of a piece to the next.

Obviously, then, we cannot start where *Music for Children* starts, but must back up and give our young students the basic training Orff and Keetman must have assumed. Why did they? They were working with hand-picked eight to twelve-year-olds who participated in the historic radio programs of 1949-53. The Schulwerk repertoire was developed and recorded, then later published. It was never conceived as a sequential curriculum, but as a series of open-ended models for music teachers to use and adapt to their own situations and folk heritages. Even in Books 1 and 2 of the American Edition, much is assumed that is not spelled out or developed step by slow step.

Two questions immediately present themselves. What basic skills do students need to have before they can learn the Schulwerk repertoire we want them to know and love? And what can we assume of our kindergarten and primary children?

For the youngest children, we can *not* assume the ability to sustain or move to a common pulse. To do two things at once. To sing in tune. To listen with concentration and discrimination. To tune into group activities with all their antennae out. To differentiate figure and ground. Or to wait their turn with patience.

We *can* assume a limited but rapidly expanding vocabulary, a fascination with words, and a basic skill in movement. They know all the obvious movements in place and in space – to pat, tap, thump, slap, clap, stretch, push, pull, twist, spin, stamp, and kick in place. They have the ability to walk, run, jump, and gallop. These movement skills, however, are likely to be almost completely on an unconscious level.

Our job is to use language to make all their necessary activities conscious, since language is the bridge to awareness, whether involving movement, rhythmic play, singing, speech play, or playing instruments. Where do we begin? We begin where the children are. Make use of their fascination with language by exploring the possibilities of speech play; make use of their impulse toward movement by exploring natural movement before trying to impose an external beat; take advantage of their delight in rhythmic play with the body rhythms that Orff so skillfully transformed into a musical vocabulary.

Children need the opportunity to play with the materials of music as a composer would. This means with speech and all its inexhaustible possibilities of inflection, tempo, meter, timbre, dynamics, and expression. They should explore their singing voices, wherever they naturally lie, in all kinds of improvisatory vocal play and in sung conversations and in story-telling, before they are expected to match pitches. They should experiment with the color and expressive possibilities of unpitched classroom instruments, in simple little rhythm pieces and sound settings for poems, rhymes, and stories. They will learn to make music before any pitched instruments are used at all.

Early training in elemental music, as Margaret Murray says, involves "a gradual externalization of the means of making music." We begin with our bodies and our voices in speech and song. Then we introduce rhythm instruments in place of our original body gestures. From exploratory movement we can proceed to the simplest structured movement, following sound signals and verbal cues. Then on to dramatic play and imaginative movement. From there we can advance to traditional singing games with simple demands – those requiring only free individual movement with no set form and no partners. Later on there are games with solo or small group assignments in set forms, usually circles or facing lines. Finally, we are ready to learn partner games.

Many adults have never learned how to move to music simply because they missed the exploratory stage of moving. They never went through the necessary rhythmic play that would have taught them. Our responsibility, surely, is to see that our children go through a sensible rhythmic sequence that will help most of them achieve what Phyllis Weikart calls "rhythmic competence" and "comfort in space."

Of course, before any ensemble play is possible, the children have to adjust to an external beat and keep it steady. It is hard for adults to realize that a common pulse is an abstraction, quite outside the experience of most young children on a conscious level. A common beat is a compromise necessary to make music together. It is a very sophisticated demand, as each individual must ignore a natural personal tempo and adjust to the group as a whole and a prescribed ensemble beat.

When the children can maintain a common pulse, ensemble music becomes possible. But we must beware of asking too much, whatever we choose to do next. A simple rhyme or tune over the pulse is all we should expect, whether we use speech ostinatos, body rhythms, unpitched percussion instruments, or bar instruments. Bilateral or alternating movement is often too demanding at this initial stage. Soon enough divided beats can be added against a continuing pulse, and then multiple beats can be introduced. Patterns with rests and independent movement come later, and as more and more tension is introduced between the accompanying parts, the kind of rhythmic polyphony typical of the Orff style will become possible.

We ought to analyze very carefully what we are asking of our students. Have we truly prepared them for the next stage? Have we figured out what new skills are involved? Have we decided the best approach? Have we taken the time to look ahead? Did we analyze the skills needed in the repertoire we're planning to use next month – and next term?

We need to work out a teaching sequence of skills in movement, speech play, singing, instrumental play that doesn't abruptly jump ahead two or three developmental stages in our hurry to reach a curriculum goal. Then again, have we set ourselves any specific goals at all? Are we planning a program of songs and pieces we like and know well and want very much to use – without going through a necessary pedagogical analysis? Objectively, we need to assess if our classes are ready for the repertoire we're giving them. Bear in mind the research findings of people like Barbara Grenoble, Dee Coulter, and Phyllis Weikart on the physical and neurological development of children. Our teaching goals should jibe with these findings at every stage. Let us resolve to take the time to analyze the material we propose to teach so that the sequential process we keep talking about really happens in the classroom. Then the Orff movement in this country can lead the way to a new appreciation of the place of music in our schools and in our culture.

A version of this essay first appeared in The Orff Echo Volume 15 Issue 2 [Winter 1983]. Reprinted with permission from The Orff Echo, the quarterly journal published by the American Orff-Schulwerk Association.

9. Speech Play: Theory and Practice

Speech is the most malleable of all our resources. No one speaks the same sentence, saying, rhyme or poem in exactly the same way. The simplest rhyme or saying has vast possibilities, and even at the initial stage of Orff training our teaching can be greatly enriched by the introduction of improvisation with speech play.

Speech play is elemental for children. It is far more important in their musical development than most of us realize, since it provides a first exposure to rhythmic and expressive sound. They already rejoice in their growing power to communicate, and they delight in the sound and rhythm of the words they know. Playground chants and songs of limited range are good evidence of this natural bent, and a good place to begin our music training.

We start where the children are and build bit by bit, as we introduce them to meter, tempo, timbre, inflection, accent, dynamics, diction and punctuation. They will discover the expressive use of silence, the form of rhymes and short poems, and the possibilities of variations in repetition. These elements of speech will carry over into singing and, to some extent, instrumental playing and movement. All as we are cultivating *musical* speech.

Folk and nursery rhymes and tales and songs have been orally transmitted by one generation to the next in every known human culture. Like other heritage resources, the rhythm, tempo, vocal color and range are inherent in the words themselves. There is no fixed meter. Thus there remains a fluidity, a flexibility, that is lost when meter is imposed. In Western culture, it took centuries for song texts to acquire inexact metrical notation, and still longer for our mathematically precise abstract signs and symbols for rhythm and meter to develop independently of spoken language. Our ancestors took over a thousand years to move from the free rhythmic speech of ancient poetry and drama to our current mathematically accurate notation.

Think of all the many variables in speech: long and short syllables; accent; duple, triple, and compound meters; timbre, tempo, dynamics, pitch, inflection, emphasis. As elements of music, as well, these can best be taught through speech play, as Orff and Keetman were wise enough to know. Speech play is a subtle resource we humans never outgrow. Our repertoire of sayings, rhymes, and stories from our cultural traditions provides an essential basis for musical development that we cannot afford to neglect. Furthermore, it's fun. The children love it. And there's plenty of room for improvisation. Why, they can learn to speak far better than many parents in this careless age.

In any Orff curriculum speech play, body percussion and movement necessarily come first, long before using the printed song settings and instrumental pieces. There are, however, only a few speech exercises included in Volume I of *Music for Children*, and they are all either translations of German texts or often unfamiliar English ones. We need to find American rhymes, poems, folk tales, and stories to supplement these traditional English nursery rhymes and stories. It's important to remember that most of the songs and instrumental pieces in Part I of Volume I were not designed for young children but rather for the older children in Keetman's demonstration classes on Bavarian Radio. Orff and Keetman had to work quickly for these broadcasts, recasting the ideas they had developed years earlier for the young-adult Güntherschule students. The result, understandably enough, is a bit of a jumble.

Too many of us assume we should begin with Part I. That seems logical, except that the basic training in Part II was meant to come first. Because the progression is not consistent in Volume I, we teachers must make the effort to fill in the gaps. We can provide the essential basic training from our own tradition, with the help of Keetman's invaluable *Elementaria,* which sets out the correct progression in great detail, and Brigitte Warner's *Orff Schulwerk: Applications for the Classroom*, a thorough and thoughtful guide to effective Orff teaching. Keetman's series of small gray books for xylophone are also essential. They are carefully sequenced and basic to understanding the intended teaching plan.

Normal English speech has a limited range: a "reciting tone" near which most of our conversation takes place; a somewhat higher range for emphasis, and a slightly lower range for less important private or parenthetical remarks. Exaggerating the vocal range beyond these bounds will sound false and phony. Meaningful speech requires a musical line and a flowing rhythm, like song, endlessly variable after the initial metrical stage. There is no single right way to say anything, but always endless opportunities for variation and improvisation.

SPEECH PLAY IN ACTION

A. Let's begin with single words in name play. I like to start by choosing four children whose names have different rhythms. For instance, David, Eleanor, Mary Helen, John. The chosen four stand in front of the class while, from behind, I tap their heads lightly, as the class says their names aloud. Later I'll repeat one name, or alternate to make varied patterns. Then a child volunteer or two take a turn in my place before we choose another set of names. You can, of course, transfer the speech patterns to unpitched percussion once the names are familiar.

Or have the children work out name dances if you wish. The names can become steps. With two contrasting names, you will have two different steps, and a longer dance. This game works equally well with lists of fish, dogs, flowers, trees, or whatever your class is currently interested in. Be sure the names always have complementary rhythms.

B. Young children need endless drill on steady beats and regular rhythms. Fortunately there are lots of traditional rhymes to practice with, many already familiar, like "One, Two, Tie My Shoe" or "Hot Cross Buns," or "Bow, Wow, Wow, Whose Dog Art Thou?" Start with simple speech play. Say and clap the beat or walk the beat while reciting the rhyme together. Later add supporting body percussion patterns to reinforce the beat. Keep the patterns easy, so every child can be successful. Start with L-R-L-R on the knees, and take a long introduction before speaking the words.

Introduce patsch-clap patterns when they're ready. Before introducing stamp-clap patterns, use marching rhymes to help the children feel the beat in their feet. Finger snaps can be omitted then added later. Here are some good examples.

First, in 2/4 time, "March, March":

> March, march, two by two,
> Dressed in yel - low, red and blue.
> March, march, three by three,
> Ma - ry, Bi l- ly, march with me

Other favorites are "Two, Four, Six, Eight," "The King of France" and "Jack and Jill," and in duple time, and "Higgledy, Piggledy," "Intry, Mintry," "Humpty, Dumpty," *etc.* in 6/8.

> The King of France
> And forty thousand men
> Marched up hill,
> And then marched down again.
> And when they were up they were up,
> And when they were down they were down,
> And when they were only half way up
> They were neither up nor down.

Young children also need experience with freer rhythms. Use imaginative texts like this, with built-in intimations of improvisation and variation:

> Intry, mintry, tribbledy fig,
> Deema, dima, doma, dig,
> Howchy, powchy,
> Noma, nowchy,
> Hum . . . tum . . . too,
> Olliga, bolliga, boo,
> Out . . . goes . . . YOU

C. With older students I like to begin with a string of single words. For instance, I have the class suggest words for ways of walking, and write them on the blackboard – saunter, plod, amble, meander, stamp, limp, shuffle, tiptoe, zigzag, march. I ask a volunteer to get up and move around the room to act out one of these words and have the class guess which one. If the word is "meander," for instance, then others can join the meandering leader until another volunteer chooses another way of walking.

Colors are great fun to play with too. People have such strong feelings about them and readily participate. I ask for color suggestions and then invite five or six students with color choices that flatter each other rhythmically to stand several feet apart. Initially I direct, with gestures that the colors' names suggest, to repeat the names in a very free rhythm – it's not strictly metrical at all. At first, the colors may be in a set sequence from left to right as the students stand in front of the class; later, I use whatever sequence I want. Volunteer directors follow, until we tire of the color combination and select another set.

People love to play this game, whatever their ages and training stage. A couple of years ago, a group chose puce and chartreuse, which are *not* among my favorite colors. It was fun to inject a good deal of feeling into the color play as I lingered on those I liked and exaggerated my dislike of the others. It is also fun to develop other word sequences – like words associated with Halloween or Thanksgiving, or for your younger students, the months of the year, birds, flowers, or fish names.

D. Older children and adults may enjoy a more demanding name game that has opportunities for a variety of accompanying body percussion patterns and amusing word play.

It goes like this:

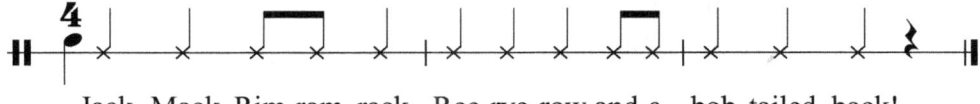

Jack, Mack, Rim ram rack, Ree rye row and a bob-tailed back!

The players sit in a circle on the floor and after the accompanying pattern is established the leader starts off with the first verse, repeating it a time or two until it's secure. Then the fun begins. Each person in the circle substitutes his/her name in the pattern. For example, if Isabel starts and Jerry follows, then:

Isabel, Misabel, Rim, ram, Risabel, Ree rye row and a bob-tailed Bisabel.

Jerry, Merry, Rim, ram, Rerry, Ree rye, row and a bob-tailed Berry.

And so on around the circle until everyone has had a turn.

Next try folk sayings and short quotations. With teachers, I like to begin with one of Orff's most important declarations: "All song must come from speech." How would you say it? What's the obvious way? How else can you say it? Another way? Still another? What does Orff mean? Jot down in stick notes three or four alternative possibilities.

Here are a few more traditional sayings and quotations to play with. Start with the obvious, then notate three alternative rhythmic solutions for each. (Remember that rests are a great invention.) Try:
- Look before you leap.
- Penny wise, pound foolish!
- Time and tide wait for no man.
- Take time while time is for time will away!
- Once is never enough.

- Some are wise, and some are otherwise.
- Work keeps at bay three great evils: boredom, vice, and need. (*Voltaire*)
- He who MUST play cannot play. (*Adam Carse*)
- Don't look back! Someone may be gaining on you! (*Satchel Paige*)

E. One of the delights of speech play is the rich vocal paraphony that results when everyone speaks in his/her own natural range, with no attempt to match pitch. But first we must find a common rhythm and inflection, so that the rhythm, voice quality and "tune" are unanimous.

Here is a nonsense, ball-bouncing rhyme I love to use with K-2 children, especially around Halloween. It's "Ungai, Mungai" (rhymes with "hung-dry"):

> Ungai, mungai,
> Alligator ungai,
> Chicka-chacka chungai,
> Over!

Take the time to explore the possibilities of the long, slow nonsense syllables as you lead the class with your voice and your gestures. Then make it all clipped and playful, with rests inserted between the words. Extend it with other nonsense lines to rhyme with "alligator ungai" if you want more variety.

Next, use it for a ball-bouncing game. You bounce the ball around the circle to each child in turn, while everyone says the rhyme aloud. Later, bounce it unpredictably, to whoever looks ready to bounce it back. Soon the children can take turns as the leader as everyone chants the rhyme. If it proves a favorite, let the class work out a two or three note tune on A G E. Add body percussion, unpitched percussion, and/or a simple bordun on bass xylophone to accompany the children as they sing the new tune. The long "ung" syllables offer endless possibilities for rhythmic speech play:

- Use echo-play, very slowly, making good use of the long "ung"s.
- Chant matter-of-factly, quite metrically, with body percussion accompaniment.
- Insert rests between the words, with a gradual crescendo.
- Repeat in canon, with two groups.
- Change the meter; make it fast and playful.
- Make up a hand-sign tune using two or three notes the class knows, and use the class tune in the ball game.
- Add bar instrument and percussion accompaniment.
- Let volunteers work out movement to match.

- Have a few recorder players alternate with the singers in playing the class tune.
- Put the whole sequence together for Halloween – or just for fun.

Don't try to do all this at once! It takes weeks of delighted play to find what your particular class most enjoys doing. And, certainly, it will come out quite differently with each class, even though the basic development remains the same. The sequence is from simple speech play to accompanied song and movement. I would also suggest that you start your own collection of rhymes and short poems that have some magic in them. Carefully pick those that deserve the same sort of extended play.

F. Another favorite for primary classes is the English rhyme, "Christmas Pudding":

> Into the pudding put the plums,
> Stir about, stir about, stir about;
> Next, the good white flour comes,
> Stir about, stir about, stir about.
> Sugar, and peel, and eggs, and spice,
> Stir about, stir about, stir about;
> Mix them and fix them and bake them twice,
> Stir about, stir about, stir about.
> Into the oven to bake all day,
> Riseabit, riseabit, riseabit.
> Out of the oven, and put it away,
> Wrap it, and pack it, till Christmas day!

The children should sit close together in a large circle to form an enormous mixing bowl! Mime adding ingredients to the pudding one by one, stirring them vigorously with an imaginary wooden spoon. Then act out wrapping and storing the pudding. (The last two lines are mine, added since the puddings should not stay in the oven indefinitely.)

G. Mid-grade or older children and even adults enjoy this endlessly variable marching rhyme that goes:

    Left__ left__ left, right__ right, Left right__, right__, right left__

Vary the position of the rests as you play with this marching chant. I heard soldiers singing it as they marched up a hill in San Francisco years ago when I was attending the Bellflower Symposium. The soldiers always used *Do* on the "lefts" and low *So* on the "rights."

You can designate different leaders, who will each devise a variation. The class joins in as they follow the leader around the room.

Encourage the students to notate it simply with L, R, and rests, like this:

    2 || L__ L__ L R__ R || *etc.*

I've also found this very useful with beginning recorder players, since any new note can be used as the "right" with an already familiar one as the "left."

Here's yet another marching rhyme for your students to enjoy, with a delightful shift of accent in the third line. It's also great fun to play on hand drums, once you work out the accentual shifts from right hand to left hand and back.

> Left__, left__, I had a good job and I left.__,
> Left my wife with twenty-four children without any gingerbread.
> Did I do right__, right__, right by my country when I
> Left__, left__, I had a good job and I left *(etc.)*

H. "The Bangalory Man" is a favorite for movement improvisation. The chosen Bangalory Man leads a line of several classmates who imitate his or her movement while marching around the room. The rest of the class chant and accompany the rhyme with body percussion and/or unpitched percussion. There's lots of room for variations in tempo, movement, and style from one leader to another.

> Follow the Bangalory man,
> Follow the Bangalory man,
> I'll do all that ever I can
> To follow the Bangalory man.

With its overlapping words, "Infirtaris" has a mysterious air that makes it unusually stimulating for mock-serious unaccompanied speech play, or a Klang-Ostinato setting. Each line may be said by a different soloist, with each speaker freezing in place until the rhyme's complete. Take your time. [*Pronunciation guide is in brackets. Ed.*]

Infirtaris,	[in fir, tar is]
Inoaknoneis,	[in oak, none is]
In mudeelsare	[in mud, eels are]
In claynoneis	[in clay, none is]
Goatseativy,	[goats eat ivy]
Mareseatoats.	[mares eat oats]

I. I like to use "From Wibbleton to Wobbleton" as speech play with a relatively complicated patschen pattern and, later, as a movement game. For the speech play, I have Wibbleton always on the right knee and Wobbleton on the left; for the movement game, stand with the Wibbletonians at one end of the room and the Wobbletonians at the other. Each side can move forward only when their town is called out, and must freeze in place when the other team's moving. Later, let both sides move on "sixteen miles" as well. Great fun when the class needs to move around for a while.

> From Wibbleton to Wobbleton is sixteen miles;
> From Wobbleton to Wibbleton is sixteen miles.
> From Wibbleton to Wobbleton,
> From Wobbleton to Wibbleton,
> From Wibbleton to Wobbleton is sixteen miles!
>
> *England*

I also like to transfer it to xylophones: "Wibbleton" and "to" on low G; "Wobbleton" and "from" on low C; "sixteen miles" on alternating G's and C's, or C's and G's.

Some of the insistently metrical rhymes, like "One, Two, Tie my Shoe," or "Hot Cross Buns" or "Jack Jim Joe" are very useful when your classes are just learning their "Taa's," "Ta-ti's," and "Taa-aa's", and need to practice writing, saying, moving and playing them on sticks, wood-blocks, claves, or drums.

J. At this stage I like to give each child an envelope of rhythm cards in duple meter and ask the class to match names, words in different categories, and short rhymes. We combine name pairs to make longer patterns; later, we form strings of names that sound well together. These can be children's names, animals, fruit, reptiles, or whatever else catches their fancy. Then we move on to Question+Answer play, *etc.*

The sets of rhythm cards grow thicker as more duple patterns are introduced. Soon we graduate to finding tunes to match the word rhythms or rhythm patterns we've chosen, or transfer them to the timpani, unpitched percussion, or the bar instruments.

K. Short rhymes like the following provide a good foundation for improvisation and composition, either by the class or solo. Be sure to start with speech play. Find many different ways to say each rhyme before settling on one to transfer to the instruments or commit to writing. Keep asking, "How else could you say it?" It bears repeating: Keep the patterns simple and complementary, whether for body percussion, unpitched percussion, or bar instruments. For example, let's play with "Rain on the Green Grass." The obvious rhythm occurs to us first:

but then:

or this:

Here are a few more examples I've enjoyed using from the vast repertoire of folk rhymes:

Red sky at night,
Sailor's delight,
Red sky in the morning,
Sailors take warning!
British Columbia

Jack, Jim Joe
Bent his bow,
Shot at a pigeon
And killed a crow.
England

I have a dog and his name is Rover,
He is the one that I like best;
When he is good, he is good all over,
When he is bad, he is just a pest!
USA

Whistle and hoe,
Sing as you go,
Shorten the row
With the songs you know.
Unknown

One for sorrow,
Two for joy!
Three for a girl,
Four for a boy;
Five for silver,
Six for gold,
Seven for a story
That's never been told.
   Unknown

It rained on Anne
It rained on Fan,
It rained on Arabella.
It did not rain
On Mary Jane;
She had a HUGE umbrella!
   England

Eenie meenie miney mo,
Catch a feeny finey foe,
Omma nooja,
Oppa tooja,
Eenie meenie miney mo!
   Unknown

Jog on, jog on the footpath way.
And merrily hent the stile-a,
A merry heart does all the way,
Your sad tires in a mile-a
   Shakespeare
["Hent the stile-a" means grab onto the stile. Ed.]

Tinker, tailor,
Soldier, sailor,
Rich man, poor man,
Beggarman, thief
Doctor, lawyer,
Merchant, chief
What about a pitcher,
Chemist, teacher?
What about a doctor,
Preacher, judge?
What about a biochemist,
Pilot, astronomer?
Singer, salesman,
Author, coach? (ADD YOURS)
   Unknown

Whether it's cold
Or whether it's hot,
There will be weather
Whether or not.
   England

For every evil under the sun
There is a cure, or there is none
If there is one, try to find it;
If there be none, never mind it.
   Unknown

Engine, Engine, number nine
Coming down Chicago line,
If the engine jumps the track
Will I get my money back?
Yes, No, Maybe so.
   Unknown

L.   A favorite of middle grade children is "I Saw Three Ships." Its variations of cargo and demands for accurate memory and interesting body percussion accompaniment are sure to be engaging. Note that "coconuts" will be first on the list in subsequent verses:

> I saw three ships a-sailing on the Main,
> Three white ships a-sailing from Spain.
> Those three ships, a-sailing on the sea
> Were bringing ten coconuts home to me.
> What were they bringing to you?

Without breaking the rhythm, each player in turn adds a new item to the cargo as the game continues verse after verse. Probably eight or ten players in each group will be enough, with each group choosing its own body percussion accompaniment. Once the children know the game, it can be fun to narrow the cargo choices to specific categories: animals, fruit, cars and trucks, *etc*.

As you plan your own word play exercises, you'll find these questions can help sort out your choices, whether you want to use the rhymes I've discussed or others. Which of these rhymes suggest playing with inflection, tempo, vocal color?

- Which suggest movement?
- Which require dramatic play?
- Which would work in canon?
- Which need a tune?
- Which need accompaniments?
- Which would work well in pairs?

SPEECH PLAY AS STORIES

Stories are a natural elaboration and expansion of some traditional rhymes. "Jack and Jill," "Humpty Dumpty," "Doctor Foster," "Three Little Kittens," or "Little Miss Muffet" are classic candidates.

One year I worked out a story for my preschoolers about Humpty Dumpty. Did you know that he lived in the little valley at the entrance to the royal palace? That his egg-people friends all love rolling around on the green grass on the gentle hill in front of the royal gate? Humpty Dumpty, who was a born show-off, was particularly skillful at rolling down quite fast and heading back up the hill until he reached a low wall. Then he rolled cautiously along the wall until he could sit proudly near the big gate. But one fine day, the royal coach suddenly came rushing and clattering, with trumpets blaring while all the egg people rolled out of the way. All, that is, but Humpty Dumpty. In his excitement, he fell off the wall just as the king and all his men swung into view....And you know the rest.

Next, a less familiar rhyme that affords an opportunity for dramatic play:

> Father and Mother and Uncle John
> Went to the market one by one;
> Father fell off,
> Mother fell off,
> But Uncle John went on and on,
> and on and on,
> and on and on ....

My five and six-year-olds had fun deciding why Father and Mother and Uncle John were going to market in the first place; what they were taking to market; and how Father and Mother both happened to fall off. Uncle John failed to notice that he'd lost them, so what happened when he finally discovered that he was all alone? Did he stay at the market all day to sell his fruit and vegetables? Did he find Mother and Father by the side of the road on his way home? Were they OK? What happened when they finally got back home? When the story line was complete, the children acted it out. There was a stick horse, a wagon suggested by long reins held by the travelers, appropriate unpitched percussion accompaniment, and an alto xylophone ostinato for the wagon's sound.

A short and simple folk tale can easily develop into a "mini-opera" at any level. With children in the lower grades, the teacher has the responsibility of keeping the accompanying patterns flowing and, usually, singing the recitative that keeps the story in gear. But the children can do the unpitched percussion patterns and whatever simple chants and songs you've worked out in class. A few will be ready for simple solos. But avoid public performances. Demonstrations are the thing, showing what's being accomplished without dinning it in, or insisting on perfection. The point is to *play* with our materials.

With older children, separate teams can work out different scenes from a familiar folk tale or story. Have them create accompaniments, movement or appropriate dances, and minimal costuming. Volunteers can work out a few recitatives, group songs, and solos to carry the story along. It seems to me far more valuable for the students to do something new and inventive than to perform a run-of-the-mill, ready-made show that has no room for their contributions, and gives only the best singers and players much to do.

My all-time favorite for this treatment is the Scottish version of "Chicken Little." I learned it from a Scottish friend when I was a child. The speech itself is so musical that it needs no mini-arias or choruses, just sensitive musical speech with simple bordun/ostinato accompaniments by the teacher and capable students. Unfortunately it's too long to include here, but it's on the AOSA video of my Denver Conference session if you want to learn it. (Carley, *Speech Play – Storytelling Plus*, American Orff-Schulwerk national conference, Denver, CO, November 1990.)

Song settings and body percussion or ensemble accompaniments can be added to a story whenever appropriate. Movement can accompany the plainest speech play. Start by simply reinforcing the beat with clapping or a clap-slap pattern. Later, divide the patschen into two eighths, so the pattern becomes "Taa ta-ti." Keep a repertoire of simple body percussion patterns from Volume I, Part II to use at a moment's notice. There are lots to choose from, and many more to invent.

Hand sign improvisation on two or three notes is the next stage to introduce, initially led by the teacher and later by student volunteers. When the children are ready, they learn to notate their tunes with stick notes and syllables, like this:

Rain on the Green Grass

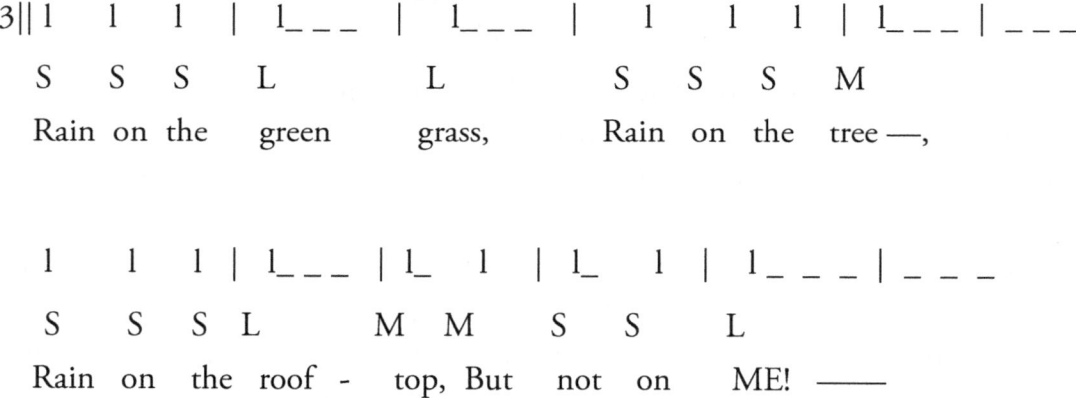

Another favorite of primary school children is my Rag Doll rhyme/story. I find that even young children are very tight and tense nowadays, and need something like this to loosen up and learn to relax.

> I'm just an old rag doll,
> I haven't any bones at all;
> I flip and I flop and I never quite know
> Just where my arms and legs will go!

Kerflip, kerflop, kerflip, kerflop,
I'm just an old rag doll . . . .
I haven't any bones at all. . . . .
And suddenly. . . down . . . I. . . . fall. . . . .
  IMC

The class lies on the floor. I go in and out among the children, lifting an arm or a leg and dropping it gently back, reminding the tense ones that they haven't any bones. Sometimes a child is so relaxed that he or she can be pulled gently over to the side, or up by both arms and then let down slowly, back onto the floor. A good example for the other children.

Sometimes a folk song suggests a story, like this North Carolina song:

Black Snake

North Carolina

One year, I developed this into a story about climbing up the mountain on an old logging road and through the overgrown woods behind our house. We went over fallen trees, through blackberry thickets, up steep muddy banks to a high meadow where the black snake lived under a big rock. One child after another teased the snake out, and then ran away. It proved a great favorite.

MORE ADVANCED EXAMPLES

Here's a useful and challenging chant for canonic movement that I learned when my husband and I were teaching in Taiwan. The text couldn't be simpler, but the game is quite demanding and definitely for older students. You'll use this rhyme:

Saa sishi saa-aa,

Saa sishi saa-aa,

Saa sishi,

Saa sishi,

Saa sishi saa-aa.

The players are divided into two, three, or four groups, by experience and skill level, with four or five players in each group. Arrange them so that all can see the leader. (I suggest beginning with two groups.)

The leader stands facing the two teams and does a simple repetitive movement pattern while saying the rhyme. Then Team One repeats what the leader did while saying the rhyme and also observing the leader's second movement pattern. When Team One is finished, the leader starts a third movement pattern as Team One imitates pattern two and Team Two starts the first pattern. And so on.

For example, you might choose to do patterns like these, ⓐ for younger children, ⓑ for older children or adults.

ⓐ

Stamp, clap, clap, slap,

Stamp, clap, clap, slap,

Stamp, clap, stamp, clap,

Stamp, stamp, stamp.

ⓑ

L together L, touch,

R together R, touch,

L together, (forward)

R together, (back)

L R L __ (in place)

The next pattern might be a series of simple arm movements; then the next, a step-jump in place pattern, *etc*. Or you could use body-percussion patterns, or simple steps sideways, or forward and back with scarves.

The term "Klang-Ostinato" simply means "sound ostinato," and there's no reason I see to postpone them to the advanced stages of Orff training. Indeed, they work well from the very beginning, especially with short poems with an element of magic.

Stories with repeated refrains provide a good opportunity for Klang-Ostinato, as in my version of "Chicken Little" in which Chicken Little repeatedly says:

> A black fairy flew
> Played nicky nicky noo
> On my silly poo.
> And I'm off to tell the King
> That Babbin's fallin'.

With plenty of time between the lines, I added a bell tree after "flew"; three taps on a wood-block on "nicky nicky noo"; a triangle on "poo"; and a hanging cymbal on "Babbin" each time the rhyme recurred.

There are many other short magical poems and a few folk rhymes that suggest the same free and minimal treatment. I suggest Edward Lear's "Far and Few" or Lilian Moore's "Until I Saw the Sea" or one of my favorite folk riddles from North Carolina:

> Green as grass, and grass it's not;
> Red as blood and blood it's not
> Black as ink and ink it's not
> What is it?
> What is it?
> (Solo) .... A blackberry!

A couple more of my favorites for older students are "Night" by Sara Teasdale ("Stars over snow...") and the final verse from "Inversnaid" ("What would the world do, once bereft of wet and wildness...") by Gerard Manly Hopkins. Take time to say the texts aloud until everyone knows them by heart, trying different tempi, adding rests if needed, playing with the rhythm, the inflection, the timbre, the dynamics, until the group finds its own way of saying it together. Then consider the available sound possibilities that seem most appropriate for your chosen text.

Keep the accompaniment thin, adding one instrument at a time to set the mood and scene. Let the texture remain transparent, so the words come through. Sometimes only occasional punctuation is enough, with one or another percussion instrument at a time. Sometimes you may want to assign a solo voice to a line or two, or repeat a meaningful line *tutti*. Sometimes an ostinato or two may be appropriate. Play with the possibilities. A setting will never come out the same with a different group, or on a different occasion.

There are very few examples of sound settings of speech in the Schulwerk. Those that are included come almost as an afterthought in Volume V in a section titled "Pieces using Speech," p. 111ff. There are also examples in the additional *Paralipomena* volume. Several examples, however, appropriate for older students and adults, are included in my edition of *Carols and Anthems from the Schulwerk II*, including two speech choirs over three timpani in **Omnia Tempus Habent** and several examples of recitative and paraphony.

When I was a girl, my mother read to my brother, sister, and me every night as soon as we were in bed. That is, except for Sundays, when Dad read poetry instead. It's amazing to remember all the books we heard and all the poetry we learned to love. It didn't occur to me till many years later that it was also a wonderful way to get us all off to bed promptly. I particularly remember the year Mother read Howard Pyle's *Robin Hood and His Merry Men* to us. Every evening, we played Robin Hood for the half hour before bedtime when we had the run of the house. Few children are so fortunate today.

Times have changed, and most children now depend on electronic sources of entertainment. So it's up to us, their teachers, to see that they're exposed to traditional sayings, rhymes, stories, games, and poems. Speech play, happily, lets us build our students' sense of the possibilities of musical speech Let me close with an urgent suggestion: Make your own collection of rhymes, poems, and stories that are particularly meaningful to you, and worth teaching to your students. Not just for today, but to remember all their lives and teach to their own children. Nothing less is worth either your time, or theirs.

A version of portions of this essay first appeared in The Orff Echo Volume 34 Issue 1 [Fall 2001]. Reprinted with permission from The Orff Echo, the quarterly journal published by the American Orff-Schulwerk Association.

10. Building the Layered Orff Ensemble

Establishing a sense of ensemble with children or adults is easiest through a gradual approach. I like to begin with inexact echoes on one note. I choose a note on alto xylophone and play a short pattern. A student player echoes it on the xylophone, alternating hands, while the rest of the class slaps the pattern on their favorite knee and sings it on the chosen pitch. Each child in turn moves up in line to play the alto xylophone and then returns to join the group. To keep it lively, keep changing the note and the rhythm, but keep it short. Also, I develop patterns on two neighboring notes; then on two thirds, *etc*. Later, use all the bar instruments available, letting children choose their own note in the C Pentatonic set-up.

After this, I introduce exact echoes on several bar instruments at the same time. Have the class begin by playing the pattern on their knees before transferring to the instruments. The next step is to introduce Question+Answer play. I repeat the same short melodic question for each student volunteer to answer with an improvised phrase, Q+A style. The children can line up at the same instrument, or they can use my bar instrument one at a time.

I recommend introducing ostinato patterns next. This is where the ensemble can come alive. Begin simply, perhaps with alternating octaves on C's or G's. Then use repeated open fifths, and after this is comfortable, stepwise patterns with alternating hands. For those pupils who can, combinations should follow. Use the ostinato to accompany a *So-Mi* chant to a familiar rhyme. Then a *So-La-Mi* setting of a rhyme with hand-sign singing. Finally, the teacher adds a solo improvisation on soprano recorder.

I like to teach simple repertoire by rote at this stage. There's no need for notation here and the ear training is invaluable. (For an example of suitable pieces, see Keetman #8 in *Erstes Spiel am Xylophon*, Schott 5582.)

BUILDING THE CARPET OF SOUND

The Orff carpet of sound can produce a magical, compelling sound without the use of magic – just layers of ostinati. Here are my two favorite guidelines:

Axiom: The fewer voices, the more each can do;

The more voices, the less each can do.

Rule: No holes in the carpet!

Remember that the phrasing is in the melody, not in the accompanying ostinati. The role of the ostinato is to sustain the momentum of the music, not to break with the phrases.

When building up an Orff arrangement for an existing melody or for improvisation, strive for rhythmic contrast between the parts, contrasting timbres, and complementary ranges. Here's how:

1. Establish the meter and tonality in the lowest voice.
2. Add a middle-range ostinato, either alto xylophone or alto metallophone, as appropriate to the material.
3. Add an upper pattern that either reinforces the melody or complements it sparingly.
4. Add appropriate unpitched percussion.
5. Add an improvised melody, or sing or play an existing melody, with combined resources.

For example, for an A G E melody, build up layered ostinati in *La* Pentatonic on A and E, and have a volunteer lead hand-sign singing. Follow that with Q+A play on alto glockenspiel in groups of four volunteers. Alternatively, build up ostinati on G and D in G Pentatonic for a lively improvised dance on your soprano recorder. Volunteers can play Q+A on soprano and alto xylophones, or play Pass-it-on with each student in turn improvising over the patterns, until the melody is finished. (The insecure can simply decline until they're ready to participate.) Note: All soloists *must* volunteer. No one is expected to improvise or solo until ready to do so. All criticism must be impersonal, or you might kill a child's impulse to play with the materials of music for life. Be sure to discuss what happened after each exercise. Ask yourself and the group:

1. What's needed next as you build the carpet of sound?
2. Do the patterns fit together? Is there rhythmic tension between the parts?
3. Are there any holes in the carpet (missing part or layer of percussion) that need to be filled?
4. What tone color should we choose next?
5. Do we need to add any unpitched instruments? For emphasis or color? For dramatic effect?
6. What would be the best choice for a solo above the ensemble?
   - Hand-sign song improvisation?
   - Solo improvisation on soprano or alto xylophone?
   - Q+A play on two glockenspiels?
   - A magical poem for a Klang-Ostinato sound setting?
   - An overture for a mini-opera based on a familiar folk tale?

This is the best way to expand your understanding of the process. You will be inviting everyone in the class to consider more deeply what works well in building arrangements. Sharing the resulting music with your students is immensely satisfying. Using these ideas as stepping-stones, you can develop with your own resources the compelling, supportive, layered sound that is the hallmark of the Orff Approach.

RECOMMENDED

- Keetman, *Elementaria: First Acquaintance with Orff-Schulwerk*, translated by Margaret Murray, Schott.
  A wonderful book, organized sequentially in every area – speech play, ensemble, and movement with innumerable fine examples for immediate use, plus full explanations of teaching procedures.

- Warner, *Orff-Schulwerk, Applications for the Classroom*, Prentice Hall.
  Excellent.

- *Music for Children*, American Edition of the Schulwerk, Books 1, 2, 3, Schott.
  Essential American repertoire for beginning Orff classes to the most advanced.

- Carley, *My Recorder Primer*, and *My Recorder Reader 1*, Brasstown Press.
  Simple American folk rhymes and songs.

- Carley, *Simple Settings I* and *II*, Brasstown Press.
  American rhymes and songs, arranged for Orff ensemble.

This essay was previously unpublished.

11. The Essential Use of Improvisation in Teaching Recorder

Improvisation can serve as a magic key to the early and rapid development of musical skill and sensitivity on any instrument. In improvisation, aural memory is trained, pitch awareness is cultivated, and a feeling for phrase and form develops naturally. Improvisation always focuses the student's attention on the musical results, since there is nothing to distract, and gives a special sense of achievement and release, even on a very simple level.

Once a player has the courage to start improvising, the pleasure in doing so can only grow. Skill and musical imagination develop side by side. The use of improvisation from the very beginning of music study leads to a much better technique and to more sensitive playing than any other approach I have ever tried. In turn, the improvisation techniques on the recorder are readily transferable from the recorder to other instruments and the voice.

The emphasis on improvisation and ensemble had from the first attracted me to the Orff Approach. In Toronto, I shall never forget Gunild Keetman's demonstration of improvisational techniques with recorders and Orff instruments, or the choral improvisation at the end of her session when the whole hall burst into song. This, I felt, was what I'd been looking for – this was a way of doing improvisation that I could use with my own students.

Thanks to a German friend, I knew about the German edition of the Schulwerk long before I ever saw or heard an Orff instrument. I found the books far from self-explanatory, and after trying some of the first volume's rhythmic exercises, I put them aside. The English (Murray) edition had the same problem and wasn't more helpful. The techniques of improvisation were really never spelled out in any of the five volumes, and only hinted at in sections of Volumes I and V on rhythm, or in a few rhymes, melodies to be completed, and scattered suggestions in the back of the books. There was no hint as far as I could tell of the extensive use of improvisation in movement training.

During my training at the Orff Institute in Salzburg in 1963-64, I also found a lack of development of the techniques of improvisation in the actual teaching process. It was specifically apparent with recorder instruction. (I understand it has changed since.) So this, then, is my own application of the techniques of teaching improvisation as I discovered in the Orff Approach, applied to the learning of the recorder.

Over the years I have introduced hundreds of classroom and music teachers to the delights of recorder playing in my summer Orff workshops. Many children and adults have had the same experience in my private classes. I have found that recorder players of any age or at any stage play more musically and progress much faster with a generous dose of improvisation. And students learn to look forward to and to love this part of their lessons, when they are allowed to play their own music in their own way.

BEGIN WITH IMITATION

Why begin with imitation? Because aural memory and inner hearing must be developed before individual ideas can be expressed. And, of course, one has to have some tonal vocabulary to work with. Also, hearing and reproducing the correct pitch with proper tonguing, hand position, and breath support comes most easily by imitation. Listening, after all, is basic.

I begin with echo play, first on one tone, then on two. With older children and adults, I like to start with C' and A, the falling third. It's the "natural chant of childhood" and the basic interval for both the Orff and Kodaly approaches. (With younger children, I begin with G down to E so both hands are involved right away.) Here, for example, are some very simple patterns for a class of beginners to echo:

To make the texture more interesting, assign a patsch-clap pattern to half the class while the other half echoes your phrases, then change assignments. Keep the patterns simple enough that most of the class is immediately successful. (This is one of the main virtues of using improvisation: You know exactly where each member of your class stands, musically speaking. No one ever improvised beyond his or her own ability!)

More experienced musicians can, of course, do more complex rhythms and longer phrases even when they are just starting on the recorder. It is up to the teacher to challenge them musically from the very beginning. I find that everyone needs a lot of practice in making up interesting tunes within a very limited range, no matter what their previous training. My little **Scherzo**, for example, uses only three notes on the recorders, a wood block, a tambourine, and a glockenspiel or soprano xylophone.

Carley, *Recorder Improvisation and Technique Book One*, Brasstown Press 2023, p. 20.

To vary the assignments, play a phrase for half the group to echo, then the other half, then *tutti*. As soon as confidence has been built up, go around the class individually, giving each child a pattern to imitate. If missed after a second try, have the whole class join in, and give that student an easier one next time. Incidentally, everyone fingers every phrase, and thinks it, until their own turn comes to play. One soon learns to match the phrase to the child's ability so that the result is usually successful at first attempt. But the teacher does need to learn to think up new patterns fast, without any interruption of the rhythm.

The next step is to let a volunteer from the class take the teacher's role, inventing, say, four phrases in turn for the whole class to echo. The word "volunteer" is all-important here, for the pupil will only fail if forced into the teacher's role before there is confidence to do it well. This stage can be helped by establishing a simple rhythmic ostinato with part of the group to support the soloist and the echo. The rhythmic accompaniment gives continuity to the effort and helps to maintain a steady rhythmic flow from one phrase to the next.

After the children have become adept at echoing simple melodic phrases, and after most of them have willingly taken the teacher's role, a new stage is reached in which individual invention is cultivated through the use of Question+Answer phrases. The teacher asks a musical question (being careful to leave it up in the air) and the pupil answers (without breaking the rhythm) using the same notes as the teacher. In echo exercises, the notes to be used in any improvisation are always introduced first.

To involve the entire class, have everyone echo the question until they know it, and then play it together for each member of the class to answer. Or have part of the group do a body-rhythm accompaniment while the rest of the class answers the question. Or add an ostinato on an alto xylophone (or other bar instrument) to encourage rhythmic flow and accurate pitch.

For example, like this:

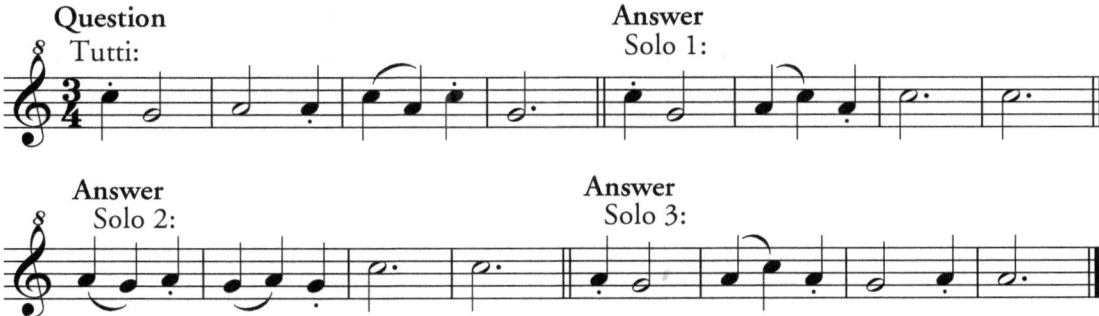

ACCOMPANYING PATTERNS:

This is a crucial stage for the development of sensitivity to phrase length, rhythmic flow, and musical sense. By this I mean the perception and use of musical motifs from the question in the answer, so that the listener is aware that both soloists are, so to speak, talking on the same subject. The teacher needs to ask many questions to make the class aware of what they're doing, aware of what makes a good question: a definite musical idea, a feeling of incompleteness, characteristic rhythm, limited range. And a good answer: continuity, usually using a motif from the beginning of the question but with a more final ending, or going on from where the question left off, to reach a definite and convincing point of repose. This is all obvious to musicians, but new to children or adults who are just beginning to "think" music.

It is very important not to interrupt or criticize until each improvisation is finished, especially at this initial stage when we need to build confidence. When the improvisation is over, ask questions that provoke self-criticism and peer judgment. The children can tell just as well as the teacher whether the questions and answers were the same length, whether there were breaks in the rhythm, whether the specified notes were used, whether the answer was a true answer, and whether the melody was happily related to its ostinato accompaniment. The occasional use of a recording device helps too, especially early in such training when children cannot remember what they did, let alone what anyone else did.

At first, the improvised phrases may be halting and unbalanced, but fluency comes with practice. When a particularly good Q+A phrase pair occurs, seize on it and teach it to the whole class. It can be the basis for further improvisation, or perhaps grist for a lesson in musical notation.

Encourage the students to find practice partners to work with outside of class. They should make up their own echo phrases and Q+A phrase pairs to bring to class, using whatever notes they're comfortable with. Some may be ready to make longer pieces and play them for the class. It is usually at this stage that the development of some system of notation becomes imperative.

When my classes start writing their own pieces down, they use a simple shorthand of stick notes and note names, like this:

There never seems to be any particular problem about transferring to regular notation. They should already be well schooled in using rhythm notation before pitch notation is introduced. (See *My Song Primer*, Brasstown Press.) Before I start them on recorders in second and third grade, I like them to have had some experience in reading and singing from a two or three line staff.

For the insecure, words can be an enormous help in improvisation, whether they're invented on the spot or already familiar. Words reinforce a feeling for rhythm and phrase length and give confidence to the tense child or adult who either peters out in the middle of a phrase or keeps interrupting to correct what's already been done. A ready repertoire of folk rhymes and short poems is indispensable in this kind of teaching, the shorter the better, like these:

Apples, peaches,	Higgledy piggledy,	Acka backa soda cracker,
pears and plums,	my black hen,	Acka backa boo,
Tell us when	She lays eggs	Acka backa soda cracker,
your birthday comes.	for gentlemen.	Out goes you!

At this stage, it is possible to begin building simple little melodies to given rhythm patterns or familiar rhymes. For instance, you can borrow the rhythm pattern from the spirited little march in Volume I of the Murray Edition (p. 62). The clapping solo might first be transferred to a hand drum or a wood block, then later to a glockenspiel or a recorder using C' A and G, always over the same stamp-clap accompaniment. Or the accompaniment could be transferred to an alto xylophone using octaves and fifths, G D' D D', *etc.*

As new notes are learned, echo-phrases introduce new connections and new tonguings. New rhythm patterns are used, first by the teacher, then again by volunteer soloists, and then all around the class. Each child should be ready for either role. Similarly with Q+A: first the teacher asks the questions, then a volunteer soloist takes the teacher's role; then question and answer are alternated all around the class. In either type of exercise, the tonal range is first set with echo exercises.

It is, of course, equally necessary to practice making up questions to fit a given answer. Often I teach an answer phrase to the whole class for them to play *tutti* in response to the improvised questions. Gradually phrase lengths are extended and new demands made. For instance, use only E G A and C' and make your answer end on A or on E, or G, or the more obvious C'. This shift in tonal center, one of the charms of the pentatonic scale, is more easily felt if reinforced on one of the bar instruments with a simple ostinato on A and E, or whatever is appropriate. For example:

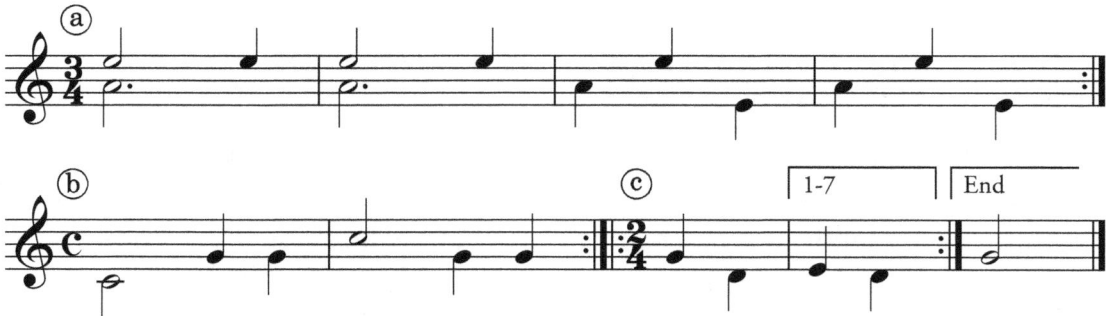

Sometimes the ostinato may be played by part of the class on their recorders, while the teacher improvises a tune above. It is also very good practice to have the children walk at an easy tempo while they're playing a simple ostinato. The movement helps cultivate a feeling for a steady tempo, and in the intake of breath, a feeling for phrasing. Simple movement patterns may also be used, particularly with children who have had previous movement training, such as four steps forward and four steps back. Or change direction after two phrases in the solo part.

Multiple ostinati can be introduced as soon as the children can hear them and stay together, using body-rhythms, rhythm instruments, Orff instruments, voices, and recorders, singly or in combination. The first step is to have the class echo and sustain a simple rhythm pattern while the teacher improvises against it, like this:

When this is successful, add another ostinato. Then transfer these familiar patterns to rhythm or bar instruments while part of the group continues to do the original body-rhythm version with the soloists. The possibilities, even at this initial stage, are endless, so don't be tempted to move along too fast. The musical ideas of repetition and contrast, of rhythmic flow, of rhythmic tension between parts, of phrase balance and the expressive use of timbre and dynamics have to be slowly absorbed.

Another useful idea is to work out simple descants to familiar songs, even at the two or three note stage. Not everyone will be able to hold a part against the familiar tune at first, but it's a good challenge for the more capable and musical in the class. For instance, here's a possible descant on soprano recorder to **This Old Man:**

As soon as low E is introduced, the song can be sung in the key of C and the recorders can transpose their part to G and E.

When questions and answers flow freely it is time to improvise longer forms. Use two questions and two answers, or combinations of echo and Q+A phrases. One of the more difficult assignments is to ask a question, wait for the answer, then repeat the same question before a more final answer is given. It requires great concentration and takes a lot of practice, even for an accomplished musician. Try it!

The four-phrase form might be used as the A section of a three-part song, with a new phrase, perhaps with a new tonal center, introduced and echoed as the B section before the first melody is repeated. Or the same little composition could be used as the A section of a rondo, with the whole class playing the theme together between contrasting, improvised episodes.

The contrasting sections should usually be the same length as the theme, but with new material and in a new mood, and with new rhythmic motifs, sometimes with a new tonal center. Volunteers might be asked to play successive phrases in a Q+A period, echo phrases, or if the theme is long enough to warrant it, in a combination of assignments. Sometimes I give very definite assignments as to form and tonality; sometimes I leave it open for the students to decide on the spur of the moment. Soon individual members of the class will be ready to improvise entire sections by themselves, and might bring full compositions to class.

Rhythm and pitch percussion accompaniments add enormously to the effect of these longer improvisations. Sometimes we begin with the ostinati, building them up one at a time, filling in the holes and playing a pattern that suits the instrument on which it is played. Simple dances can be worked out, with solo dancers or small groups improvising the contrasting sections in movement, just as the recorder players are doing. The movement thus clarifies the musical form while it adds a new dimension to the improvisation.

The same techniques of improvisation are used as new notes and new scales are introduced. First the C D E G A pentatonic, then the D E G A B pentatonic and the C D F G A pentatonic, including, of course, the minor pentatonic and other possible tonal centers. Later the major scales are introduced, one at a time – G, C, F, *etc*. Then the minor modes are explored in turn (Aeolian, Dorian, Phrygian) both in their natural positions and transposed, until the whole range of the recorder is mastered and the flavor of each scale has been explored.

Improvisation on the recorder is also used very extensively in movement lessons as the teacher plays for walking, running, or skipping, or for listening games, or for simple singing games and dances. When the children have a secure range of even three or four notes they may also begin to take part in improvising for movement. They can accompany the class's movement, or determine it, by the nature of their improvisation. Larger spatial forms are gradually developed along with longer musical forms. Sometimes the movement follows the music, sometimes the music accompanies the movement, but always it's an intimate symbiotic relationship, each element dependent on the other.

I urge you to experiment with these techniques at your own level, whether you have anyone to work with or not, whether you are a teacher or a student. There is no pleasure to compare with that of making your own music, improvising in your own way.

A version of this essay first appeared in The Orff Echo Volume 7 Issue 2 [January 1975]. Reprinted with permission from The Orff Echo, the quarterly journal published by the American Orff-Schulwerk Association.

12. Hand Drums: Playing Techniques and Repertoire

Choose a drum with a tunable skin head if at all possible. It will last longer than the less expensive substitutes, and provide far more variety of sound than those with smooth plastic heads. If you must substitute, find a drum with a textured plastic head. Some dealers also carry lighter-weight wooden drums that have leather heads with tunable keys at considerably lower prices than the top brands.

I much prefer the tuning pins right on the drum, so that instant adjustment is possible depending on the weather or the particular piece you are playing. For class use, the inexpensive treated-paper heads are a necessary compromise. But, if at all possible, try the drums yourself before buying them, since some sound much better than others. A twelve-inch drum is the most versatile.

Hand drums are played in many styles and traditions in different parts of the world and kinds of music. I will discuss three basic techniques here. These are developed at greater length, with other methods, in my book, *For Hand Drums and Recorders*.

ONE: STANDING TECHNIQUE

Support the drum by the four fingers of the non-dominant hand with the thumb resting on the upper surface of the rim, slightly off-center and away from the body. The larger the drum, the higher it must be held to allow for the full extension of the playing arm for the thumb-stroke — about a quarter of the way up from the bottom rim. The smaller the drum, the lower it must be held. Look in a mirror and check your position before you begin to play.

The thumb-stroke, used for accent and emphasis, is played with only the side of the first thumb joint striking the drumhead with a sudden flick of the wrist. An immediate rebound allows for the greatest possible resonance. The rebound, led by the wrist with the hand relaxed, returns the hand to the starting position, slightly higher than the player's head. The playing hand describes a skinny figure eight on each stroke. There should be no feeling of effort in raising the playing arm if the rebound is properly used and the arm is fully extended.

The finger-stroke is played at the rim with the wrist almost opposite the supporting wrist, comfortably above the rim. The stroke is a flick of the wrist that brings only the fingertips in contact with the drumhead. The fingers move together in a relaxed position, but fully extended. Normally, one plays with only the two longest fingers, but more may be added as dynamics require.

Practice thumb strokes separately and slowly until you can produce a dependable *pizzicato* sound. Avoid swishing the thumb along the drumhead; swinging the playing hand out beyond the rim of the drum; sticking out the thumb to make contact with the drum; choking the drum so it is too high for a free thumb-stroke, or allowing the drum to twist sideways.

When alternating thumb and finger strokes, the rebound will be somewhat shorter, and should carry the playing hand right into position slightly above the drum. Try playing familiar rhymes such as "Pease Porridge Hot" or "Baa Baa Black Sheep" with all the accents as thumb strokes, and all the unaccented syllables at the rim with finger strokes, using only the first joint of the playing fingers.

This technique is identified as "HD I" and notated on two staff lines, the upper for the finger strokes and the lower for the thumb, as in the following examples.

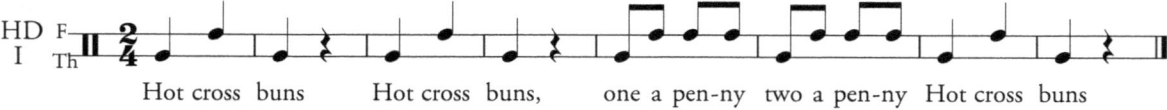

Then try these two canons:

Jack Jim Joe

Isabel Carley

Maria

Gunild Keetman (taught to IMC by Lotte Flach)

Ma ri a come, Ma ri a, come, Now come and see I have a new red ball for you Ma ri a come, Ma ri a, come, Now come and see I have a new red ball.

TWO: FINGER TECHNIQUE

The second style of playing requires holding the drum in the same way as before, but the player may either stand or sit with the drum resting comfortably on the knee and the playing hand comfortably cupped, ready to play in the closest quadrant of the drumhead. When standing, the drum is held comfortably higher than in Technique One. The thumb plays about two inches or less in from the rim, with a nice lively rebound. No wrist flip is necessary. The patterns pivot between the thumb and the middle finger, with other fingers added as necessary, always leading back to the thumb for the next accent to avoid awkward shifts of weight and direction. The fingers are played where they fall on the drum head in a relaxed position, with a springy rebound. The tone should be much lighter than the thumb stroke so that a real contrast is perceived. This technique works well for ostinati.

The notation for finger technique uses as many lines as fingers. When all five fingers are required, staff paper serves perfectly, with the thumb assigned the bottom line, the forefinger, the second line, *etc*. Try improvising over any of the patterns below, singly or in combination.

Here is a Playford dance that requires the use of Techniques One and Two:

Jenny Pluck Pears

Playford, 17th c.

Learn **Peas an' the Rice** securely before doing it as a two-part round.

Peas an' the Rice

Work Chant

Peas an' the rice, Peas an' the rice, Peas an' the rice, done, done, done, done. New rice and o-kra,

Eat some and left some. Peas an' the rice, peas an' the rice, done, done, done, done.

THREE: AMBIDEXTROUS TECHNIQUE

The player sits forward on the chair, knees bent, with the drum held between the legs at about a forty-five-degree angle. Twelve-inch diameter drums with tuning pins are best, with the tuning pins caught in the angle of the drummer's knees for stability. The player must be prepared to lean forward and back as the drum part requires, to get arm weight into the thumb strokes and a lighter touch at the rim for the finger strokes. In any case, be sure to strike the same spot on the drumhead whichever hand is playing, to ensure the same tone and resonance.

Practice the thumb stroke first, slowly, alternating hands. The thumb stroke is similar to that used in Technique One. There's a last-minute twist of the wrist to bring the fleshy pan of the first joint in contact with the skin, and an instantaneous rebound, either to allow the other thumb to play or to bring the hand up to the rim. Practice the following exercises, and invent more of your own.

Then practice the finger stroke at the rim, alternating hands and rebounding fast enough for the other hand to play in exactly the same spot. Play in the middle of the drum with only the first joint of the second and third fingers, except in unusually loud places. Try the exercises here and make up some more.

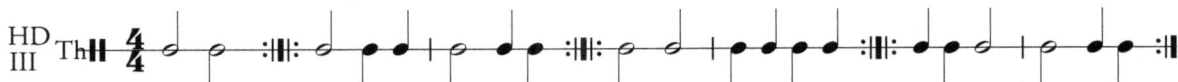

84   Making It Up As You Go

Then try this, alternating hands consistently.

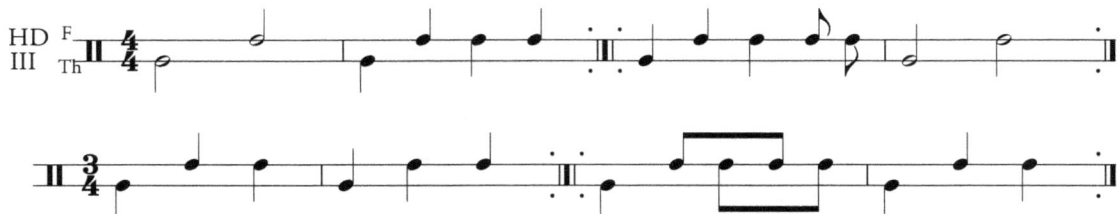

Below, play **Dance for Recorder and Drum**, from my book *Recorders Plus*, published by Brasstown Press. (See the next page for how to build a rondo with it.)

Dance for Recorder and Drum

Isabel Carley

Turn the dance into a rondo. Here is one possible way:

> [C] Improvise a new section over a new Drum Ostinato and return to [A].
>
> [D] Improvise on soprano recorder and return to [A].
>
> [E] Improvise on hand drum and return to [A].
>
> At [B] only the right hand plays, with the thumb and fingers near the rim.
>
> *n.b.* The drum part serves as an introduction if you repeat the first four bars.

HAND DRUM REPERTOIRE

For further instructions and a selection of pieces from the Medieval period and the Renaissance, folk songs and dances, and original compositions designed for recorders and drums, see my book, *For Hand Drums and Recorders*, published by Musik Innovations.

I also recommend Gunild Keetman's two books, *Für Flöte und Trommel I* and *II*, published by Schott. These are full of delights for solo or group performance with older children and adults. Schott has also published *Alte und Neue Tänze* by Bergese (Ed. 3573), including a Fourteenth-Century Estampie and works by Orff and Keetman. Consult the Murray Edition for such pieces as **Marmotte**, p. 28, **Allegro**, p. 84, and a demanding solo for soprano recorder and drum on p. 78, all in Volume IV.

Many short pieces in the Rhythmic sections of both Volumes I and V in the Murray Edition work well on drums. Those already notated on two staff lines – especially the canons and pieces for stamping and clapping – are easily read as drum parts. Adapt the others by assigning all the accents to the thumb, whichever drum technique you use. There are neglected pleasures here that you can bring to life with hand drums, particularly when your older students lose interest in body percussion.

Effective drum parts are found in the three volumes of the Rohr-Lehn series, *Vortragsbüchlein für die Schule*. Timpani or tambourine parts can transfer to hand drums, and the recorder parts are well chosen for intermediate players of soprano (Book I and II) and alto recorders (Book II and III) with optional percussion parts in all three. This is excellent repertoire in skillful arrangements.

My favorite repertoire comes from the Medieval period. When all that survives is the barebones tune, we are free to make our own appropriate arrangements using voices, recorders, lutes, guitars (very sparingly), tuned bells and drums (as pictured in the manuscripts and sculpture of the period).

Portions Copyright 1994 Carl Orff Canada Music for Children / Musique pour Enfants. A version of this article originally appeared in the Winter 1994 issue of Ostinato (Volume 20, No. 2) and is reprinted with permission.

13. Music Plus: Kindergarten Curriculum Goals

This curriculum of eleven developmental elements was proposed in 1981 and revised in 1990, part of a book project that remained in manuscript form at IMC's death.

1. Provide basic rhythm training through movement, speech, singing, and instrumental play.

Rhythm training will include: individual movement exploration, both in place and in common locomotor movement; practice in following a common pulse through body rhythms, movement in place, and locomotor movement; participation in rhythmic activities in response to sound cues, instrumental accompaniment, verbal cues, rhymes and poems and/or songs; responding to sound signals; participating in set singing games in a variety of floor patterns, both as leader and follower; improvising new ways of doing familiar activities.

2. Develop the musical use of speech.

Speech play encompasses: training in using single sounds that many children find difficult (long vowels, consonants, and blends); echoing *exactly* spoken words, names, and rhymes, using a variety of inflections, tempi, dynamics, vocal timbre; accompanying rhymes, sayings, and short poems with vocal ostinati; asking and answering questions in a context of melodic improvisation and for any voice pitch; dramatic play; moving in response to verbal cues, names, rhymes, poems; using speech patterns as rhythmic building blocks; abstracting rhythm patterns from the corresponding speech patterns; making independent rhythmic compositions. All of these activities focus on the musical qualities of speech and the concepts, which transfer to music training *per se*. Scope for individual experimentation and leadership when the children are ready is provided, while cultivating respect for and enjoyment of the spoken language and our oral tradition.

3. Develop aural memory.

Through echo play in speech exercises; with body rhythm play; using rhythm instruments; by singing in a very limited range. This develops a sure sense of similarities and differences, gradually extending the aural memory. Focus narrows to pitch perception and performance accuracy, whether singing, playing, or participating in a singing game. Cumulative songs, response songs, narrative songs build memory and concentration – which, of course, carry over into other educational areas.

4. Develop aural discrimination.

With echo-play in speech and song, and a variety of listening games, the recognition and differentiation of sound sources in a classroom – objects, body rhythms, vocal sounds, found instruments, unpitched percussion, pitched bar instruments, piano, recorder – are enhanced. Movement in response to different sound sources develops awareness of timbre and of sound quality. The first classroom instruments are introduced along with the use of the teacher's hand signals; these are used for color and punctuation in oral stories and settings of poems. All the instruments are introduced one by one for movement response, and then put into the children's hands for specific assignments – as signals, for color, as substitutes for familiar words, in little rhythmic compositions; also as sound and silence, pulse and pattern, solo and group-independent ostinato patterns.

5. Develop the singing voice.

Improvisation is used from the very beginning as children learn to find their own voices and sing in a comfortable range. Later, tone-matching games are introduced, pitched where the children are able to sing. Only then are they expected to match pitches in the limited range songs on *So-Mi* or *So-Mi-La*.

Folk songs have been classified into several different categories to clarify what is expected: *Limited range songs* are for everyone to sing as accurately as possible; *Response songs* are for the teacher to sing to the class, with the class joining in on the (very simple) responses; *Sing-along songs* are songs in a limited range that most children can sing spontaneously as a group or with minimal teaching; *Activity songs* are for the teacher to sing and the class to respond to as the lyrics suggest; *Singing games* are for the teacher to sing and the children to respond in traditional forms, singing if they are able to do so; *Resting songs* are for the teacher to sing to the children when they relax after active play.

6. Develop basic instrumental techniques.

Good technique with the basic body-rhythm gestures provides the foundation for all subsequent instrumental play. Unpitched percussion instruments are used sparingly and with specific aesthetic intent and correct technique from the beginning. Knee-slapping exercises prepare for the introduction of the xylophone and glockenspiel later in the year; they are used to support the singing voice in simple ensemble settings. Instrumental play moves from our first instrument, our physical body, to simple percussion instruments played with the hands and fingers, then on to instruments played with mallets – a gradual externalization of means. All three stages help develop large muscle movement before small muscle control is needed for the demands of conventional orchestral instruments.

7. Develop visual, kinesthetic, aural, and verbal imagination using a variety of multi-sensory experiences, particularly through the use of dramatic play.

The growing minds of kindergarten children will develop inventiveness and creativity, applicable all their lives.

8. Develop taste, independent judgment, and divergent thinking.

Materials are carefully chosen that are worth remembering for a lifetime and meet the standard that children would someday want to teach them to their own grandchildren. Rhymes, poems, stories, games, sayings, and songs are selected for their own intrinsic worth, not simply for pedagogical purposes. Real choices are presented, so that children can begin to make their own decisions about what is effective and which resources to use in a particular context. Almost all the material comes from the North American folk heritage or from recognized poets and storytellers.

9. Reinforce academic learning.

Coordinate with academic preparation through rhythmic games and in a play context, particularly in Language Arts and the use of numbers.

10. Make the child's introduction to formal education in kindergarten a joyous experience.

A child's first year in school is an opportunity to establishing a multi-sensory foundation for all future learning.

11. Serve as a model for a wider school curriculum, not just applicable to the kindergarten year.

Tie together rhythmic activities throughout a child's schooling to build a cooperative, creative, accretive, cyclical, multisensory educational experience.

14. Advice to Orff Teachers

Let's start with what we know as Orff teachers. In their spontaneous play, children become totally involved with movement, speech, chant and rhythm. The Orff Approach begins with play and leads students into a carefully sequenced exploration of musical elements. This builds their musical understanding, with an emphasis on the process, not performance. Our focus is on participation rather than skill development; on developing musical ideas rather than reproducing fixed forms. Broadly put, it is music education devised from the viewpoint of a composer.

Carl Orff claimed only three special elements for his approach: the basis in speech play; the use of a special group of instruments with removable bars, suitable for children and appropriate for either solo or accompanying parts; and the practice of improvisation. I think he took for granted two more: the use of movement to clarify musical structure (and other concepts) and the teaching value of his own historically-based monodic style that transcends Western harmonic music.

With all this in mind, here is a brief guide for practicing teachers and a conceptual foundation for professional courses for teachers-in-training.

FIRST EXERCISES

I like to begin my ensemble sessions with a variety of improvisational exercises, whatever the ages and stage of the class. A good exercise is the following. First set up the scale you want to use. Ask the children to count off into teams of four, six, or eight. The basic idea is that each child will play an improvised melody and then hand off to the next player. A tremolo on the last note, very quietly, is the signal for another to start his or her improvised melody. When the last team member finishes, all join in on the final tremolo with a gradual crescendo followed by a gradual diminuendo until the sound disappears.

Then it's the turn of the next team. No rules beyond that, but it's wise for you to start off each group yourself. (Should someone get carried away and go on too long, remind the children to keep their tunes in proportion to the others in the team's set.)

As time goes on, you can suggest picking up an idea from someone who has already played, or play "next-door neighbors" in stepwise tunes. Students can be encouraged to use skips or repeated notes, or make a lively tune or a sad one, a lullaby or a march. As students listen more and more attentively, their improvisations improve in musicality and should become more closely related to each other. You want them to reach for increasing levels of aesthetic satisfaction.

Another exercise I like to try from the very beginning is an "inexact echo." I ask the class to play back whatever I play in the same rhythm, the same style, and same phrase length, without worrying about using the exact same notes. If I play stepwise figures, they do too. If I play two notes at a time in parallel movement, they do too. If I play figures with repeated notes, they do too. In this way the students build up their own technique and their aural acuity and memory. Soon some of them are matching the notes as well, at least part of the time.

POINTS TO REMEMBER

- You should keep looking for new rhymes, poems, sayings, and new songs, patterns, themes, and new spatial forms. Encourage your pupils to contribute new material.

- Introduce them to pentatonic tunes, *i.e.*, those omitting the half steps (fourth and seventh degrees) of the major scale, to songs from your school series, and to pieces from the *Music for Children* Volumes.

- Flexibility, imagination and simple materials used in depth are at the core of this approach. Exercise them repeatedly in different ways. The goal is not to cover some specified curriculum, but to take the time to explore possibilities for accompaniment, for movement, for extension, for variation. For your pupils, the result is the basic repertoire will be *really* learned and *really* retained.

- Here's a strong reminder. Never let the children do more at a time than they can hear. Initially, accompanying patterns must be extremely simple, with body percussion and rhythm instruments purely reinforcing the underlying pulse. It is harder than we expect for young children to do two things at once, or to hear two things at once. If the ensemble is not exactly together, go back to preliminary exercises that use body rhythms and movement and further simplify the arrangement. Keep the texture thin, so that everything is *heard*. If the children forget to sing, simplify.

• The accompanying patterns should progress so slowly that students can do them almost automatically, with complete muscular freedom. You will soon discover which children can handle the more independent parts and which become tense and break the rhythm, except on the easiest ones. Very often it is the slow learners who excel at free rhythmic play, whether in movement or in instrumental play, and the brightest children who cannot relax enough to participate freely, at least until they learn to trust their muscles and ears.

• Remember, *all* the suggested patterns need not be done at once. And of course you may add or substitute new variations that you and your class invent, using the same notes.

• There should be some improvisation in every lesson, whether with words, movement, rhythm patterns, percussion instruments, voices, or pitch instruments. Begin with "copycat" games and don't go too fast. Let the children *volunteer* to take the teacher's role or to solo. Forcing a solo assignment before a child is ready can only result in tension and frustration.

• Always this is key: hearing and doing come first. Reading and writing music should happen only after all the elements are familiar. Then it is simply a process of recognizing something that the class has already clapped or sung or played. It is far more critical to develop musical concepts through speech, movement, note singing, and playing than it is to rush the class along into learning notation. Use your own judgment about introducing charts. When you feel your students are ready, add that element of visual perception to their already-developed aural and muscular skills.

CLASSROOM CLIMATE

If any creative work is to be done, a climate for growth is necessary. In the classroom this means that you as the teacher must feel free and relaxed, willing to let children learn from their mistakes – and that you are calm enough to learn from your own.

When it comes to improvisation exercises, give a definite assignment within definite limits, and then leave the children alone. Don't interrupt or criticize while an improvisation is played; afterwards, lead the class in constructive criticism by asking questions. Did it fulfill the assignment? Did all the phrases feel the right length? Did it sound finished at the end? Which answers were most satisfying? Why? What was the form? These questions and answers should affirm where the student has made progress, not belittle the effort or discourage trying again.

Again, a relaxed atmosphere is essential. No one can improvise freely where there is impatience, tension, or authoritarianism in the air. What the Orff Approach has established is that only in improvisation can you really tell what your pupils can do. Trust this. No one has ever improvised beyond his or her own ability!

You need to sense how the class is advancing. Self-confidence and muscular skill develop in small steps. Children know when they're ready for a new challenge. Let them volunteer. Above all else, remind yourself that whenever you force the issue, you defeat your own purpose.

MUSIC AND MOVEMENT

Although Orff acknowledged his debt to Dalcroze in the use of movement in music education, here the emphasis is on *basic* movement or what any normal child can do naturally, without dance training. This is not a superimposition of movement on classical compositions, but the development of music and movement together. With practice, the children will make their own music to accompany their own movement routines.

One aspect of movement training is unique to the Orff Approach. This is the use of body rhythms as a percussive instrument. Clapping, stamping, finger snapping and knee slapping (often called by its German name, "Patschen") are combined into complex patterns and integrated in song arrangements, rhythmic compositions, and instrumental pieces. Body rhythms wonderfully provide new material for early training in improvisation and composition, while opening the way to music reading and writing – since rhythmic notation is ordinarily the easiest to introduce.

Such training takes a great deal of time and space, patience, and ingenuity, and cannot be hurried. But it is worth it. (Despite the misgivings of unimaginative school administrators.) Not only does movement training for children cultivate muscular control and rhythmic security, but it also takes musical concepts to a new dimension. Tempo, dynamics, phrasing, and form can be felt and visualized in many different ways. Through movement a feeling for ensemble can first be experienced, and rhythmic movement is also one of the best ways to solve rhythmic problems.

Incidentally, I have found it helpful to introduce beginners to movement in a game setting of "Simon Says" or "Who can…?" to avoid the sort of self-consciousness that even young children may exhibit. You may prefer some other approach.

MOVING TO THE NEXT LEVEL

Once your class has mastered a number of songs, go back to the old favorites and transpose them to other keys (D, F, G Pentatonic), repeating movement and reading lessons as needed. Introduce new songs by rote long before you develop them in depth.

Different classes will respond very differently and will need different emphases. Keep track of each class so you have a record of achievement, including the best original songs and settings, and encourage the class to illustrate them.

If you're short of instruments, SING. There are always pitch patterns that lend themselves to vocalization. Substitute solo voices for instruments in melodic improvisation. If you don't have Orff instruments yet, use what you do have and adapt the patterns to fit. (Melody bells may be substituted for both glockenspiels and metallophones, and autoharps for string drones. But there is no acceptable substitute for xylophones or percussion instruments.)

You can employ more body-percussion accompaniments, more unpitched percussion, more movement and speech exercises. Singing should come to the fore (except in instrumental pieces) while the instruments remain *accompanying* instruments. Many of the *Music for Children* songs are completely satisfying in themselves, without the use of pitched instruments of any kind. But the children will be deprived of the full musical benefits if you neglect Orff instruments entirely. These are *real* instruments whose magical sounds fascinate everyone, and for music making with young children there is nothing that compares.

See to it that every child is included and challenged at an appropriate level, and value all student contributions. Musicality is not simply another reading skill or a laborious cultivation of various kinds of physical dexterity. It is the joy of real creative music making in the classroom. These are only some of the basic building blocks. You and your pupils can put them together. Let's hear original music streaming forth from schools everywhere.

This essay was previously unpublished.

15. Transformations

With the Orff Approach, transformations occur all the time. One thing changes into something else, in a spontaneous and unpredictable way. Things never comes out the same another time or with another group. A simple play-rhyme from Ohio playgrounds turns into a mysterious chant as the nonsense words are chanted and extended beyond the obvious original sing-song ball-bouncing incarnation. A rhythm pattern is transferred to rhythm instruments, transformed from percussive body rhythms to the higher level of abstraction of the rhythm instruments. Then it's again transformed into a dance, as half the class works out movement to accompany the original rhythm piece, and a new, improvised section is developed spontaneously to extend the activity.

A short poem is learned through imitation, with insistence on a whole series of precise echoes, playing with the various musical concepts involved – inflection, tempo, dynamics, timbre, meter – until one favorite way is discovered. Then speech and ostinati are added, and perhaps some instrumental color to set the mood and support the text. It is only a short step to the melodic transformation of the original poem and the transfer of the supporting patterns to pitched instruments or vocal ostinati. A story is told, acted out by all who choose to participate. *Leitmotifs* are seized upon, whether in speech, or on rhythm or bar instruments; transitions are improvised on the bar instruments. Little spontaneous "arias" or recitatives occur. Parts are assigned, exchanged, developed; instrumental accompaniments, interludes, postludes, are worked out by different groups, and soon an entire mini-opera has come to pass, as one thing led to another and was encouraged to grow. Whether for performance or not, the idea has taken hold. It's been allowed to grow to its full extent, as far as all the participants can take it.

Of course, sometimes ideas fall flat. In that case, the leader presents another, always hoping for the magic moment when the thing comes alive and carries everyone along with it.

The same process can occur when we work with songs, settings, and instrumental pieces already in print. We can look for possibilities of extending them, of underlining their unique qualities with sensitive additions of instrumental color, of transferring them to movement and set dances, of stringing them together into larger suites or entire dramatic situations. Maybe it can pull together into a single unit the set pieces and songs that were taught separately. Transformation is not quite so obvious here, but it occurs nonetheless. For example, a whole playground sequence is worked out with clapping rhymes, jump-rope rhymes, counting-out rhymes, follow-the-leader songs, and ball-bouncing songs. Imagine "Toodala," "Little Bird, Little Bird," "Did You Ever See a Lassie?" "Left Right Chant" and a couple of simple instrumental pieces as Prelude and Postlude to the whole show.

It is not only the materials with which we work that enjoy these transformations. People transform too, both teachers and children, as this kind of immediate involvement with the materials of music and imagination takes place. New relationships develop as children learn to cooperate in accomplishing what none of them could do alone. Self-respect flourishes, as peers take seriously each other's tentative suggestions.

I have seen a child so accustomed to failure that he cannot allow himself to try, gradually lose his inhibitions and learn that he's good – really good – at something for the first time in his life. I have seen a competitive child who expects to be the best at everything learn that classmates she considers dumb can excel at improvising, while she does not.

I have seen a group of often-hostile children from different backgrounds learn to cooperate, to listen to each other, to become a human group as well as a musical ensemble. They learn there's more to their friends than they suspected; but more important is the discovery that there's more to themselves. They learn to listen to an "inner voice," to follow the melody of their own invention where it wants to go, to take dictation, as it were, from the subconscious. They fill the holes in the carpet of sound when they're making accompanying ostinati – sensitive to the sounds, to the ensemble, to the people around them.

Children who are not academically gifted may discover a talent for movement. For playing rings around their straight-A classmates. For learning and remembering melodies and patterns. For improvising rhythms and tunes and adding a new dimension to the group's achievement. This is the way sensitivity and cooperation grow. Together, they recognize what is unique to their group.

In this approach, one thing leads to another in a delightfully spontaneous, unpredictable fashion. The same rhyme or song may recur again and again, sometimes in successive lessons, sometimes not for months or even years. Each time it's different, drawing to itself different settings, extensions, and contexts. The children's aesthetic judgment and experience add more and more possibilities for evolution and transformation. I'm continually surprised at some of the hardy perennials my students keep asking for, sometimes years after their first introduction. Anything we teach in depth, allowing for individual suggestions and contributions, will stay with children all their lives. They will have been transformed.

Portions of this essay first appeared in The Orff Echo Volume 22 Issue 4 [Summer 1990] and Volume 6 Issue 1 [November 1973]. Reprinted with permission from The Orff Echo, the quarterly journal published by the American Orff-Schulwerk Association.

Part Three

Exhortations

The side trips are what we remember, both in travel and in the classroom. The single day in all the years of my childhood music classes, when we were allowed to make up a song, is the only one I remember. That day, the expected lesson was forgotten and we were encouraged to make our own music.

IMC in "On the Value of Side Trips"

16. Training: Once Is Never Enough

When I was trying to find room in my filing cabinet for last summer's notes, I came across notes I'd taken in Toronto twenty years ago and was shocked and surprised to discover how much had escaped me at the time, only to be hard-won years later. It took repeated exposure to the Schulwerk, first in the year-long course at the Orff Institute, then in further workshops and conferences, and still later in my own teaching and composition. This experience convinced me that a single immersion in the Orff Approach in a workshop can never provide adequate professional training, no matter how good the student or the course.

That is why I feel so strongly that we are making a serious mistake in allowing absolute novices to enter our certification courses, which are (or should be) designed for those who are already committed to the Orff Approach, not those who are trying it on for size. There is still a great need for short introductory courses to precede the Level I courses that are increasingly offered all over the country. But there seem to be fewer every year now that it's a matter of prestige to have a local Orff Certification Course.

In my experience, it is the students with extensive previous Orff training on top of a solid musical education, plus some teaching experience, who benefit most from our certification courses and are prepared to do distinguished work. Without any of these prerequisites, students are severely limited; lacking most, they are dangerously handicapped. And under so much pressure – bombarded by too many new stimuli all at once – that the experience is altogether too stressful to be productive.

Probably the best way to get professional training in the Orff Approach would be through in-service training, with constant interplay between course and classroom. This is seldom possible, for lack of permanent Orff faculties in our departments of Music Education. Our summer courses do have the advantage of multiple faculty, brought in from all over the country – at least at the more prestigious schools – but this can also be overwhelming to a novice, since all of us have developed our own styles, our own approaches, even our own sequences. It's a rare course that really coordinates the entire curriculum. This wealth of viewpoints is enormously enriching and stimulating to an experienced student, but quite beyond a raw initiate.

The unsynchronized multiple approach can only be confusing and deeply discouraging in our certification courses (as at our National Conferences) and succeeds all too often in eliminating from our ranks those promising novices who are just not yet ready for the experience. How many were lost because of our plunging them into a professional course for which they were totally unprepared? And how many courses have had to be seriously watered down to accommodate novices who should never have been admitted in the first place? The two needs – for introductory courses and for solid professional training – are quite distinct and should be kept separate if either kind is to be truly effective. It is simply not possible to do both at once.

One week is quite long enough for a first immersion in our revolutionary approach to music-teaching. After a year's assimilation, those who have a natural affinity for this style of teaching will be ready to tackle a demanding Level I course with confidence and understanding. Perhaps we should all follow Denver's lead and require at least a week's previous Orff training before admitting anyone to our professional level certification courses.

Quite by accident, I discovered a most successful schedule for a Level I certification course if it proves impossible to require a preliminary course. Divide the Level I course between two summers. The intervening school year is used to assimilate the first summer's teaching and the students are rarin' to go when they return to complete their Level I training. The slower tempo gives them time to grow and to readjust to this new style of teaching without the appalling pressure that usually develops in the second week of our certification courses. The students have already absorbed all they can and need time off, not more material and more demanding assignments. With such a divided schedule, the students were able to absorb far more than if they had slogged through the entire course the first year.

Those few who have already completed their certification sequence at another school and are willing to start over prove to be our outstanding graduates. As time goes on, I trust that there will be more and more such adventurous souls who dare to continue their education after their piece of paper has been won. To venture into strange territory, repeating as many levels as they can afford under new teachers. Content and materials vary amazingly from one course to another and from one teacher to another, even though all of them may be conscientiously following the official AOSA Guidelines. The usual two weeks per summer for three years is scarcely time enough to master a whole new approach to one's profession! One learns more by seeing different applications of the same philosophy than by proceeding with only the minimal basic training that most of our certification courses now provide.

The need will increase for advanced seminars for serious Orff teachers who still feel the need of further training. There is more interest every year in the Level Four seminars I proposed five years ago. Each participant brings a contribution, and sharing becomes possible on one's own level, without having to hold back so as not to dominate the class. That often has happened to our best students in certification courses.

Established professionals feel the need just as strongly as these eager young people, and such small-scale encounters provide an ideal opportunity for mutual stimulation, since the mix of people and ideas will never be the same twice. The universities are not likely to sponsor such seminars, since there is so little money involved in a course deliberately limited to twelve or fifteen people, but I'm convinced that they will yet flourish. Every year makes more people eligible, and the cream of the crop needs stimulus and encouragement even more than the average graduates of our professional courses.

Whatever our level of expertise in the Orff Approach, all of us need the stimulus of repetition, encountering old materials in a new context. The Schulwerk, as Orff himself said, is never finished. Neither should our study of it be. There is always more to discover, more to learn, more to apply in our own teaching. Each repetition of anything of value brings new meaning and understanding as it bears the weight of our growing experience and skill, so that our perception of what is ostensibly the same thing has actually changed since our last encounter. Each repetition becomes a far richer experience than its predecessor, no matter how often we revert to the same material and explore the same sequence. Once is never enough.

A version of this essay first appeared in The Orff Echo Volume 15 Issue 4 [Summer 1983]. Reprinted with permission from The Orff Echo, the quarterly journal published by the American Orff-Schulwerk Association.

17. Music Worth the Difference

After the first fine foolish rapture of enthusiasm, when the realities of crowded classrooms, crowded schedules, inadequate equipment, and unreasonable demands from the administration and PTA have worn us down – and the repertoire we learned at our Orff workshops is depleted or found too difficult – it is tempting to give up and wonder why we ever chose to try something so new and so demanding. The old emphasis on performance – which probably dominated our own musical educations – comes back to the fore. How can we resist, when there's no time to think between classes, no music room, no space to move, no relief from the pressure for results?

In the first place, take your time. Don't attempt too much too soon. The basic stage cannot be skimped, whatever the age of pupils you work with. Squeeze the juice out of what you choose to do. If it's worth doing, it's worth exploring in depth, in different dimensions. "How else could we do it?" is the basic question, but it is useless until the children know the song or piece by heart.

Once learned, the fun begins. What other instruments could play the tune? How could we make the form clearer? Could you whistle it instead? What could we add to emphasize the rhythm? What could we omit? Could we add a new instrument on each repetition and make a long crescendo out of it? Which part would make a good solo? Could you play it again on different instruments? How could we make it longer? How could we change the character of the piece? (Change tempo; change the scale; change timbre.) What sort of movement would fit the mood (a) by yourself in place, (b) with a partner, (c) in a small circle, (d) in opposite lines? How can the movement pattern in space make the musical form clear?

Keep coming back to the favorite pieces of each class, but with a difference each time. It is only when music is completely assimilated that interpretation is possible at any level of music-making. It is far more important to have musical experiences than to get through a set number of songs that scarcely anyone will remember next week. Only the best repertoire we know can cultivate the kind of sensitivity, imagination, and taste we aspire to nourish in our students.

In our age of complexity, simple music has an added charm. We owe a great debt to Carl Orff in that he perceived the richness of simplicity, opening our eyes and ears to the endless possibilities in the use of basic music for children's musical education.

Improvisation in the teaching itself is elemental to the Orff approach. Take your time and do only what you feel free to do. If you go too fast, you'll let the old performance bugaboo out of the bag. It is not pressure but release in creative work that our children desperately need. Don't let your inhibitions, or your impatience, deprive your children of the joy of making music in their own way. Let music become an illumination and a lasting resource in their lives. It takes courage and confidence in your students and in yourself; but given that commitment, there is no limit to what you can do together.

A version of this essay first appeared in The Orff Echo Volume 1 Issue 3 [June 1969]. Reprinted with permission from The Orff Echo, the quarterly journal published by the American Orff-Schulwerk Association.

18. Ersatz Orff
(And How To Avoid It)

I remember very vividly when I was in Salzburg being peripherally included in a conversation with Dr. Orff and Professor Keller about a new series of books that had just been printed. They incorporated some of Orff's ideas and techniques, and were beautifully printed with delightful illustrations in three or four colors, a handsome job of book-making. The pages looked fine, with Orff instruments properly arranged on the page, one part on top of another. But Orff was really upset, calling attention to this and that, pointing his finger at one flaw after another. Obviously he felt that the whole undertaking was a complete travesty of his approach to music education. I was then too much of a novice to see at a glance what was wrong, but I kept wondering how anything could *look* so right and be so wrong.

Now that music publishers in this country are aware that we are here to stay, that the Orff Approach is not just a fad, a passing fancy, we are facing the same problem that Orff faced in Germany and Austria in the 1960s. There are very few publishers who take us seriously enough to have knowledgeable editors sift the wheat from the chaff. We are increasingly going to be confronted with handsome imitations of the Orff Approach that do more harm than good. They will seize on obvious gimmicks and completely miss the sequential development and the style.

Yes, they might use the Orff instruments – sometimes in strange combinations with other instruments. Or they make odd substitutions, as if the choice of tone color and combinations of instrumental ostinati were of no importance. They treat pentatonic scales as if they were simply incomplete major scales, and afflict them with inappropriate cadential harmonies. They seize on melodic motifs from the tunes they are accompanying, so that the ostinato completely disappears when the same spot in the tune is reached again. I have never found that in any arrangement by Orff or Keetman. They equate ostinato and phrase, so that the Orff carpet of sound – the supporting bordun-ostinato texture – has large holes in it at every phrase ending.

What can we do about it? It seems to me that we need to be very alert to the quality of the material we use, to analyze and study it thoroughly before we introduce it in our classes. Nowadays, this is sometimes difficult, since so few music stores keep any sort of adequate stock available for examination, but at least we can order new publications on approval and judge for ourselves at our leisure.

Here are some of the things I would look for:

1. Is there a respect for the scale of the melody? Does the arranger limit the accompaniment to the notes of the tune?

2. Is the tune itself appropriate for an Orff setting? There are, for instance, many pentatonic tunes which are indeed gapped major scales, with so much emphasis on scale tones which disturb the underlying tonality that they are quite unsuitable.

3. Are the accompanying patterns complementary? Do they flatter each other? Is there rhythmic tension between them? Do they involve contrary motion? (Except, of course, at the paraphonic or shifting chord stage.)

4. Are the bar instruments sensitively chosen and appropriately used? Does a xylophone have a moving part without sustained notes? Or is it foolishly assigned long notes more appropriate to a metallophone or a glockenspiel?

5. Are the instruments used with restraint? No more and no less than the particular setting can best employ? Fat scores are often an indication of poor taste. Simplicity is one of the hallmarks of the Orff Approach. There is far more skill involved in leaving out nonessentials than in using everything available.

6. Are the unpitched percussion instruments used effectively for color? For rhythmic impetus? With restraint, so that we will not tire of them?

7. Is there a clear understanding of the style appropriate to the stage of development in the Orff sequence? For instance, is cadential, functional harmony reserved for use with full diatonic major or modal scales? Or is it inappropriately introduced with pentatonic or hexatonic melodies better suited to bordun-ostinato accompaniment?

8. Are the texts worth learning? Worth teaching? Worth remembering? Unfortunately, there are all too many smarty texts in current use, which betray a lack of respect for the children for whom they are intended. With the wealth of folk rhymes and poems, of folk tales and well-written stories, there is no excuse for short-changing the children we teach – particularly in an approach based on the sensitive use of speech.

9. Does the melody bear up under close scrutiny? Is it clear formally? Are the phrases related in a pleasing way? Is there a climax? Is the range appropriate to the age and stage of the children? Is it rhythmically interesting, no matter how limited the range?

10. Is it musically satisfying? Is it worth the effort? Will it provide a permanent enrichment for the children you teach? Will they remember it with joy?

A version of this essay first appeared in The Orff Echo Volume 13 Issue 4 [Summer 1981]. Reprinted with permission from The Orff Echo, the quarterly journal published by the American Orff-Schulwerk Association.

19. On Teaching Styles

In the last few months I've come across several articles on Learning Styles. Visual, auditory, and kinesthetic learning styles are differentiated, along with corresponding preferences: for a quiet atmosphere or constant background sound; for solitude or group participation; for blocks of time or short, interrupted spurts of concentration; for bright or subdued light; for a straight chair at a table or desk, or a soft chair, or on the floor. The list goes on and on. Every effort is made to help the classroom teacher spot the natural styles of their students and to find ways of encouraging their natural bents in a regular classroom. Rather a tall order!

And then there's the additional distinction between the left-brain dominant children (with their logical, sequential, verbally-skilled analytical minds) and the right-brain dominant ones (with their spatial and kinesthetic gifts, who think in Gestalts, from the whole to the parts, and who often become impatient with standard sequences). Until about the age of eleven, when the two "brains" are abruptly separated and hemispheric specialization develops, children automatically use both in everything they do. After that, special efforts and techniques must be introduced to keep older children in touch with their natural artistic abilities and deepest feelings. It is up to us to find ways to reach them, as children are rarely able to understand what's happening. We want to help them learn to trust themselves – and us – so they can still exercise their gifts at this painfully self-conscious stage in development.

Given the challenge of all these student learning styles, it seems to me imperative for us teachers to figure out what our own learning styles are, our own habitual ways of planning and teaching. Probably most of us unconsciously teach much the way our best teachers taught us, using a style that comes naturally without much thought. So, do we always approach our lessons in the same way, moving from one part to the next until we can put the whole thing together in class? Do we always ask for analysis of patterns and forms and for critical appraisal as we go along? Are we intent on completing the assignment we've chosen and miss the serendipitous contributions the students are ready to make? That's left brain.

Or do we naturally introduce a new undertaking in the entirety and then move on to work out the separate parts? Do we teach more by eye than ear, comfortable only with a visual record of everything? Do we emphasize theory more than practice? Are we naturally kinesthetic, always wanting to transfer every activity into movement to make it really secure? That's right brain.

Like it or not, our teaching style is likely to miss at least half the class! How can we afford to use the same approach all year long, when this might leave out such a large proportion of our students? No wonder the success rate in teaching music in the schools has been so paltry, with the result that there are few communities where adults love to play music all their lives.

Traditionally, music has been taught as a left-brain subject like any other, a logical, visual, theoretical discipline – except when the curriculum is interrupted by performance preparation. The most extreme example of this I ever encountered was about twenty years ago in Puerto Rico where my family worked one summer. It was my responsibility to teach basic musicianship and theory. Most of the local participants had no previous exposure; their learning was completely aural, so four members of my family taught each of the four parts by example. I learned from my local mentor that their traditional approach to music literacy required students to study solfège for two or three years before they were allowed to utter a sound. No wonder students were convinced reading music was a difficult and arcane skill! (They soon learned otherwise from us.) Yet back home, the avowed goals of music literacy in the schools have produced, until very recently, no better results.

We Orff teachers are lucky. Our approach mixes all the various styles of learning, so that a child most at home with movement has kinesthetic experiences, a child who learns through visual stimuli has simple written materials, and a child who learns best aurally can learn aloud by rote. Even better, all the children exercise all their faculties, learning some things one way, some another.

It is possible to teach movement through visual diagrams and verbal instructions, though demonstration and imitation are more effective for many. It is possible to teach repertoire through notation, although many learn better by rote. It is possible to teach speech patterns and compositions from the printed word, though this provides no clue to the musical elements of speech. It is also possible to teach the same elements through kinesthetic means, or simply by ear. And it is possible in all cases to teach either from the parts to the whole, or vice versa.

Perhaps we need, first, to recognize our own natural teaching style and then deliberately shift gears to other ways. That may at first seem very strange and make us feel quite insecure. But when we realize that a third to half of our class is missing out, it seems high time to start teaching to include all the visual, aural, and kinesthetic learners – instead of teaching mainly to those whose learning style is most like our own.

A version of this essay first appeared in The Orff Echo Volume 14 Issue 4 [Summer 1982]. Reprinted with permission from The Orff Echo, the quarterly journal published by the American Orff-Schulwerk Association.

20. The Value of Side Trips

As the Orff Approach begins to take its place in the mainstream of music education in this country, we need to work out a practical curriculum for use in public and private schools. The job needs doing, as we all know, since so few teachers have the time to study and analyze the skills and repertoire in all the areas we at least attempt to include. It is an overwhelming undertaking, to interweave all the aspects of the Orff Approach while welcoming the spontaneity and choice essential to musical taste and understanding.

For example, we can concentrate so exclusively on the logical progression that there is no input from the children at all, nor any choice left for the teacher. Instead of engaging the whole person, such a logical curriculum appeals almost exclusively to the left brain, and all the creative right brain skills are either omitted or minimized.

Piaget pointed out: "Anything is understood only to the extent that it is reinvented." Also: "When we teach too fast, we keep the child from inventing and discovering for himself." Or, as Maria Montessori put it: "Every useless aid given a growing organism arrests development." Children have all their lives before them. Why must we hurry them along to reach *our* goals instead of allowing them time to find their own? Must we short-change the children by neglecting time to play with all the materials at our command?

Do we offer them excursions into:
- Heritage rhymes, sayings, stories?
- Children's literature and excerpts from the great writers of our traditions?

- Movement exploration in place and in space – alone, with a partner, with a small group?
- New sound settings for speech and movement using all the unpitched instruments available to us?

Can the children explore the bar instruments one by one – at first to make sound effects, or as an interlude between scenes in dramatic play – long before a finished performance is expected?

Do we take time for short melodic explorations within very limited ranges, both vocally and on bar instruments, thereby creating the need for notation to record their inventions?

Each class can in this way identify favorites and notate them in a class book, instead of simply doing what the teacher has chosen for the next PTA performance. Perhaps this is not the time for a performance at all, but for a demonstration of what you and your children actually do when they're learning music in your classroom. Chances are, it would be much more meaningful to the children themselves and to their parents than another prepared show that makes you and the children tense and constrained. Perhaps you can at least try to perform only when the performance serves your curriculum, and plan to use repertoire you would teach anyhow, without having to detour for seasonal material. The more you can include some element of spontaneous play in the programs you schedule, the more effective and memorable they will be, and the truer to the Orff philosophy.

Another hazard, it seems to me, is the oversimplification of the layering technique that Orff and Keetman used so skillfully in their own compositions. The wonderful carpet of sound they used to support their melodies is frequently reduced to two patterns that coincide with the melodic phrase, rather than camouflaging the phrase breaks with overlaps that keep the texture alive. Too often, these carpets of sound are full of ugly holes! Too often, the patterns are the same, whatever the tune, the mood, the tempo. The stock pattern (usually with alto xylophone alone, or alto xylophone and alto glockenspiel using only open fifths on the tonic scale and interrupted by rests) like this:

Worse, this pattern is often divided between the two instruments, so neither pattern has any rhythmic continuity. What a travesty of the Orff Approach's emphasis on rhythmic motion to develop rhythmic security on the bar instruments. Continuous momentum is essential to any such growth, and interrupted patterns prevent it.

Furthermore, it's no fun doing these rest-filled exercises. There is no chance to relax into the hypnotic pleasure of playing an ongoing pattern, however simple it may be. Rhythmic movement is a delight to the human animal, and Orff was wise enough to make it an essential part of his approach. Indeed, it was his perceived need for such training that brought him to music education in the first place.

Another problem that concerns us all is how to involve the three kinds of learning in every classroom: visual, aural, and kinesthetic. The Orff Approach is the only way I know that intrinsically involves all these mode of learning. We begin with the kinesthetic and aural and add the visual as needed. However, as time goes on, the visual aspect – reading and writing and the resulting performance – is increasingly emphasized. With so little time for music in most schools nowadays, there is danger of minimizing or even omitting the aural and kinesthetic aspects of our music making. All students lose, either from the rejection of their natural mode of learning, or particularly for the visual learners, from missing the aural and kinesthetic training they so badly need.

It may be tempting to imitate other approaches to music, with their neat curricula. Requiring, for example, that only quarter-notes and rests should be used in the music class for months on end. But can we be so set in our ways, when every class is different, and moves at its own pace? Is it so important to keep everyone in the same school or state or nation doing the same thing at the same time? Or can we accept the tempo of each class and discover and teach accordingly?

Of course we do need carefully spelled-out curricula to refer to, to check with, to see how our classes compare. But we shouldn't need to follow slavishly, denying our own judgment and choice, and denying our students the excitement of exploration and discovery. We can learn to refer to them as maps, and enjoy choosing our route to the goals we share. We Orff teachers needn't resemble cross-country travelers who tear along one interstate after another, noticing the country we're traversing only when looking for a gas station, food, or a motel. Such travelers do reach their destinations, but think what they have missed along the way! In taking time to enjoy side trips and byways and unexpected serendipities, travel can become a joy.

Side trips are what we remember, both in travel and in the classroom. The single day, in all the years of my childhood music classes, when we were allowed to make up a song, is the only one I remember. That day, the expected lesson was forgotten and we were encouraged to make our own music. Perhaps we can learn to allow time for the unexpected, the spontaneous, the playful possibilities that are within our reach if we have the courage and wisdom to grasp them. Children have plenty of time. Why rush them to keep up with our impatient adult imperatives?

This essay was previously unpublished.

21. Create or Perform?

In recent years, many speeches, articles, books, and several large-scale government projects have promoted creativity in the arts. There remains a lot of misunderstanding among parents, school administrators, and music teachers themselves as to the value and practicality of creative work in the school music class. The battle was won a generation ago in teaching art, so that children today are trusted to use their own eyes and taste, no matter how strange the results may appear to adults. When art skills are allowed to develop gradually, an appreciation of the world's artistic heritage can arrive over time.

Creativity in music is much more of a problem. Music by its nature can never be a totally private undertaking. Experimentation with sound and movement should have place in class instruction before serious group music making is attempted. This takes time and patience, and careful planning. It also takes a certain attitude on the part of the teacher, as nothing genuinely creative can emerge from an atmosphere that is tense, critical, or impatient.

In all the writing on the subject of creativity in education I have seen, the role of the teacher's personality has rarely been discussed, except in an old book by Rudolf Steiner. He explains the influence on children of different personality types, and even predicts the type of chronic physical ills that will afflict pupils in middle age as a result of their teachers' personalities! Perhaps he goes too far, but unquestionably he has a point. Nothing can grow to healthy maturity in an unhealthy climate. The climate of the classroom is the teacher's doing. Is it a place where a child can grow? Or does the teacher simply play it safe and do what he or she thinks is required?

This is a real problem for those aspiring to teach the Orff Approach. We are expected to provide musical entertainment for school groups at the drop of a hat, and at least in my town, for any civic group that invites us. The pressure is enormous, and it is easy to forget Orff's basic tenet that participation is more important than performance. If we do forget, we are cheating the children and betraying the inclusive humanizing spirit of the whole approach.

I will concede it is better for children to be pushed into perfecting and performing Orff arrangements, designed by one of the great composers of our day, than to prepare a more conventional concert. Those who are selected undoubtedly gain in musical understanding, and the rhythmic training and ensemble experience are invaluable. But what of the rejects? What musical training do they get? It's the old story of exploiting the good kids and excluding everyone else. Is this education?

But, and a very large "but" it is, a performance is not the goal. It is all too easy for those of us brought up with this false emphasis to fall back into old habits. When we are on the spot and our whole career is open to public censure – as it is every time we perform or allow our classes to perform – of course we want the result to do us credit. Do we force our ideas on the children or do we use theirs? Do we stick to the printed repertoire or adjust it to our situation? Do we work out new ideas with our pupils and use those ideas in our public appearances? Do we trust them enough to ask them to improvise in public?

The need to create is basic and universal. To deny it is to frustrate the children entrusted to us. Surely there is enough adult-imposed pressure in the rest of the curriculum nowadays, without carrying into our music programs. It's the false standards of our society: that music is entertainment and the goal of music education is public performance. The human need to make something of our own and the power of music are denied in this narrow view. Every human being needs some kind of creative outlet. Failing to find this outlet results in frustration and aggression. As Erich Fromm has said: "Violence is the outcome of the unlived life. The only answer is creativity."

Other cultures and civilizations have taken music much more seriously as a means of education. For the Greeks, it was central, embracing as it did the arts of poetry, drama, and dance. Plato said "Rhythm and harmony penetrate very deeply to the inward places of the soul, and affect it most powerfully, imparting grace."

The Orff Approach regains this recognition of the basic humanizing value of music. The goal is not the cultivation of technical skills, but of imagination, of taste, of understanding, and of sensitivity. What other subject in the curriculum can do as much?

Portions of this essay first appeared in The Orff Echo Volume 1 Issue 2 [February 1969] and Volume 6 Issue 1 [November 1973]. Reprinted with permission from The Orff Echo, the quarterly journal published by the American Orff-Schulwerk Association.

Resources

Biographical Sketch – Isabel McNeill Carley

Isabel McNeill was born in December 1918 in Chicago. She grew up there and in Toronto. She received a BA in 1939 from Queens University, Kingston, Ontario, an MA in Music History from the University of Chicago in 1941, and began doctoral work the following year. While in graduate school she founded the University Recorder Ensemble.

In 1943, she married James Carley, then taught music in Quebec and Missouri schools while he was serving in the US Army. She later joined him at his post in Alamogordo, New Mexico, where two children, Elizabeth and John were born. For the next ten years, they lived in New York, Oregon, and North Texas, while her husband's career as a professor of sacred music took shape. The family moved in 1953 to Indianapolis, Indiana, along with a third child, Anne. In 1973 her husband retired, and they relocated to the mountains of western North Carolina where they lived for the next thirty years.

Isabel Carley's professional career was recharged in 1962 when she attended the first Orff-Schulwerk course in Toronto. The next academic year (1963-64) she completed an intensive one-year course of study (taught in German) at the Orff-Institute in Salzburg, Austria, earning a Specialist's Diploma with Honors. She also studied composition privately with Carl Orff. In the late 1960s she was one of the co-founders of today's American Orff-Schulwerk Association (AOSA). She served on the AOSA Board, edited *The Orff Echo* (1968-1983), and contributed to the AOSA Recorder and Curriculum Task Forces in the 1990s.

In recognition, AOSA established the Isabel McNeill Carley Library in 1985, and in 1998 presented her the AOSA Distinguished Service Award.

She devoted herself to her work as a music educator and composer for sixty years. She led Orff certification courses in the United States and abroad, teaching workshops for AOSA chapters and Title III programs, participating in national and state-level Music Educators National Conference (MENC) events, and presenting sessions at national and regional AOSA conferences.

Throughout, she taught music privately to children and adults in the US and, during 1985, in Taiwan. As a performing musician, she sang alto, and played recorders, keyboards and percussion and provided arrangements of Medieval repertoire. Retiring from active teaching in 2004, she moved with her husband to Maryland where she died in July 2011.

Her published works include numerous compositions for recorders, Orff ensemble, piano, voice, and percussion. Her best known instructional series, *Recorder Improvisation and Technique* was re-issued in 2011 in refreshed editions, along with this new book of collected essays, some reprinted and others published for the very first time.

Music & Instructional Works by Isabel McNeill Carley

COMPOSITIONS and EDITIONS

Year	Title	Publisher	Instrumentation
1962	Eleven Miniatures • Early Piano Recital Pieces	Galaxy; Brasstown Press	Piano
1963	Fox and Geese	Summy-Birchard	Solo beginning piano
1966; 1994	The Magic Circle: 81 Activity Songs and Singing Games for Young Children	J. Fischer; Waterloo	Singing and Activity Games
1968; 1990	Holiday	J. Fischer; Brasstown Press	Beginning piano piece
1969; 4th ed 1980	A Song Primer	Brasstown Press	Voice, Body Percussion, Orff Instruments
1970	Recorder Improvisation and Technique Book One	Brasstown Press	Voice, Recorders, Orff Instruments, percussion
1972	Simple Settings – American Folk Songs and Rhymes with Orff Ensemble Book 1 (CDEGA Pentatonic)	Brasstown Press	Voice, Orff Instruments, percussion
1972	Carols and Anthems from the Schulwerk I (Editor)	Schott	Voice, Recorders, Orff Instruments, percussion
1972	Carols and Anthems from the Schulwerk II (Editor)	Schott	Voice, Recorders, Orff Instruments, percussion
1972	Sing for the Joy of Easter	Concordia	SSA with optional bass
1973	Carols with Instruments (arr. IMC)	Concordia	Choir with Orff ensemble
1973	Flemish Dance Carol (arr. IMC)	Concordia	Unison choir w Orff ensemble and optional sopranino recorder
1974	Simple Settings – American Folk Songs and Rhymes with Orff Ensemble Book 2	Magnamusic / MMB	Voice, Orff Instruments, percussion
1974; 2001	Recorders Plus – Original Pieces for Recorders and Orff Instruments	Brasstown Press	Recorders, Orff Instruments, percussion
1975	Recorder Improvisation and Technique Book Two	Brasstown Press	Voice, Recorders, Orff Instruments, percussion
1976 / 1990	More Love (Shaker, arr. IMC)	Augsburg Publishing House	Treble voices w Orff instruments
1976	Recorder Improvisation and Technique Book Three	Brasstown Press	Voice, Recorders, Orff Instruments, percussion
1977	On This Thy Holy Day	Augsburg Publishing House	Unison voices with Orff instruments
1977	Music for Children Orff Schulwerk American Edition Book 2 (Contributor)	Schott	
1978; 3d Ed 1986	My Recorder Reader 1	Brasstown Press	Soprano Recorder, Voice, Orff Instruments, percussion
1979	My Recorder Primer	Brasstown Press	Soprano Recorder, Voice, Orff Instruments, percussion
1979	My Recorder Reader 2	Brasstown Press	Soprano Recorder, Voice, Orff Instruments, percussion
1979	Theory Papers for C Recorders	Brasstown Press	Soprano Recorder
1979	Berceuse for Alto Recorder Solo and Alto Xylophone	Brasstown Press	Alto Recorder and Alto Xylophone or Guitar
1979	Simple Gifts (Shaker, arr. IMC)	Augsburg Publishing House	Unison treble voices with Orff Instruments
1980	My Recorder Reader 3	Brasstown Press	Soprano Recorder, Voice, Orff Instruments, percussion
1980	Music for Children Orff Schulwerk American Edition Book 3 (Contributor)	Schott	
1981	The Night Before Christmas (arr. IMC)	Helicon / European American Music	Speech Choir and Orff Instruments
1981	That First Christmas Day (Stanzas by IMC; Chorus from Louise Larkin Bradford's Sing It Yourself; arr. IMC)	Choristers Guild	Two-part voices with Orff Instruments and Violoncello or Guitar
1982	Recorders with Orff Ensemble I	Schott	Recorders, Orff Instruments

Music & Instructional Works by IMC

Year	Title	Publisher	Instrumentation
1982	Music for Children Orff Schulwerk American Edition Book 1 (Contributor)	Schott	
1982	Amazing Grace (arr. IMC)	Augsburg Publishing House	Two-part voices, Soprano Recorder, Orff Instruments, Violoncello
1983	For Hand Drums and Recorders	Musik Innovations	Recorders, Hand drums and percussion
1984	Theory Papers for F Recorders	Brasstown Press	Alto Recorder
1984	Recorders with Orff Ensemble II	Schott	Recorders, Orff Instruments
1984	Recorders with Orff Ensemble III	Schott	Recorders, Orff Instruments
1984	Life Up Your Eyes	Augsburg Publishing House	Choir and Orff Instruments
1984	Festive Peal	Augsburg Publishing House	Choir and Orff Instruments
1985	Recorder Improvisation and Technique (Chinese / Taiwan edition)	Brasstown Press	Soprano Recorder and Orff Ensemble
1986	Shepherds, Rejoice (Shapenote, arr. IMC)	Choristers Guild	SA Voices with Orff Ensemble
1986	Wasn't That A Mighty Day?	Augsburg Publishing House	Choir with Orff ensemble
1986 / 1993	Summer Suite – Allegretto, Andante Cantabile, Circle Dance	Joseph A Loux	SAT Recorders and Percussion
1988	The Christmas Star (Folk Carol, arr. IMC)	Choristers Guild	Unison voices w keyboard, Orff instruments
1989	Suite on Four Notes	Joseph A Loux	S/T Recorder with Keyboard or Continuo
1990	A First Folk Song Suite – Old Joe Clarke; Hot Cross Buns Theme and Variations; When the Train Comes Along; Oats, Peas, Beans Jig	Waterloo Music / Brasstown Press	SR SR and piano
1990	Sing We Noel / On Christmas Night	Augsburg Fortress	Choir with Orff ensemble
1990	Suite in C – Intrada, By the River, Badinerie, Gigue	Brasstown Press	Alto Recorder and Piano
1991	Mountain Carol	Choristers Guild	Choir with Orff ensemble
1995	Carley Recorder Series: Á La Claire Fontaine – Theme with six Variations;	Waterloo	Soprano Recorder and Piano
1995	Carley Recorder Series: Silly Suite – Songs from Nova Scotia: Paddy Backwards, Old King Coul, The Quaker's Courtship, The Crocodile (arr. IMC)	Waterloo	Soprano Recorder and Piano
1995	Carley Recorder Series: Suite Québecoise – Ah, Si Mon Moine Voulait Danser; The Huron Carol; A Saint Malo; En Roulant, Ma Boule Roulant (arr. IMC)	Waterloo	Soprano Recorder and Piano
1995	Carley Recorder Series: Simple Suite – March, Scherzo, Quiet Song, Dance Rondo	Waterloo	Soprano Recorder and Piano
1995	Carley Recorder Series: C'est La Belle Françoise - Theme with Five Variations	Waterloo	Soprano Recorder and Piano
2000	Renaissance Dances for Dancers Young and Old (with CD)	Warner Bros. Publications	Piano, Recorder and Orff Ensemble, Dancers
2000	Medieval and Renaissance Dances for Recorders, Dancers and Hand Drums	Memphis Musicraft Publications	Recorders, Hand Drums, Dancers
2011	Recorder Improvisation and Technique Book One Fourth Edition – Beginning with the Soprano Recorder	Brasstown Press	Recorders, Orff Ensemble
2011	Recorder Improvisation and Technique Book Two Third Edition – Intermediate for Alto and Soprano Recorder	Brasstown Press	Recorders, Orff Ensemble
2011	Recorder Improvisation and Technique Book Three Second Edition – Advanced – Composing, Arranging, Analysis	Brasstown Press	Recorders, Orff Ensemble
2011	Making It Up As You Go • Selected Essays – Writing about Music, Improvisation and Teaching	Brasstown Press	

VIDEO

Year	Title	Publisher	Notes
1990	Video: Speech Play – the Magic of Words (1 hr 21 min)	AOSA	AOSA National Conference, Denver, CO November 1990
1990	Video: Speech Play – from Speech to Song (1 hr 8 min)	AOSA	AOSA National Conference, Denver, CO November 1990
1990	Video: Speech Play – Storytelling Plus (1 hr 30 min)	AOSA	AOSA National Conference, Denver, CO November 1990

RECORDED MUSIC

Year	Title	Publisher	Notes
2000	Music CD: The Carley Consort • Volume I – Christmas	Chenille Records	Live recordings, 1968, 1969, 1972
2001	Music CD: The Carley Consort • Volume II – In Performance	Chenille Records	Live recordings, 1969, 1972

Brasstown Press Editions

Isabel McNeill Carley Orff Essentials Collection

   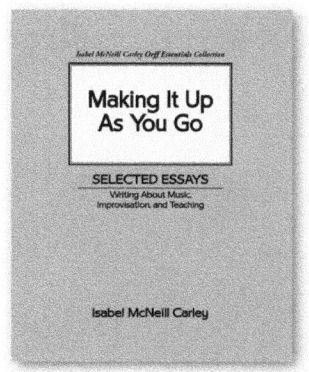

Eleven lessons for beginners and their teachers that explore C, G, and F Pentatonic and related modes on the soprano recorder. 46 songs and introductory exercises.
wire-o ISBN 978-1-931922-46-3
paperback ISBN 978-0-9836545-0-6

Building on RIT One, RIT Two transfers soprano fingering patterns to the alto recorder and introduces hexatonic and diatonic major and minor modes. 52 songs and intermediate exercises.
wire-o ISBN 978-1-931922-07-4
paperback ISBN 978-0-9836545-1-3

For the student already proficient on both C and F recorders. These lessons parallel the material in the Orff Schulwerk (volumes III and V). 46 challenging songs for advanced students.
wire-o ISBN 978-1-93192208-1
paperback ISBN 978-0-9836545-2-0

IM Carley's written work from over thirty years. The essays are grouped in three sections: Origins, Practicum, and Exhortations. Includes biographical sketch and list of IMC's publications.
ISBN 978-0-9836545-3-7

IMC's Five Little Books

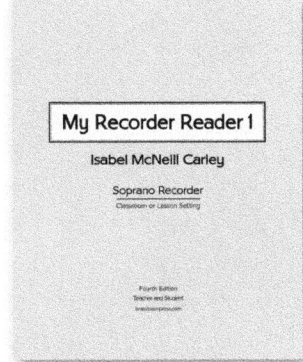  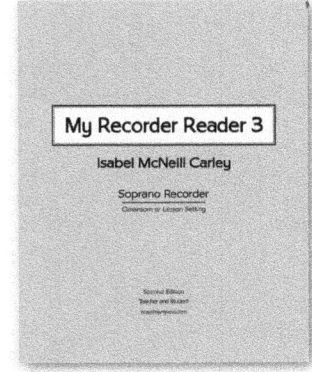

The three **My Recorder Reader** books are a coordinated series of songs to bring a student from elementary playing to a more experienced level. Notes are added one by one to extend the student's range, with minimal instructional comments. The carefully graduated sequence of the pieces facilitates individual mastery and skill development.

41 Songs in G Pentatonic Scale and Modes.
ISBN 978-0-9836545-6-8

47 Songs in C Pentatonic and F Pentatonic.
ISBN 978-0-9836545-7-5

44 Songs. Expanded ranges, Pentatonic to Diatonic.
ISBN 978-0-9836545-8-2

EBOOK!

 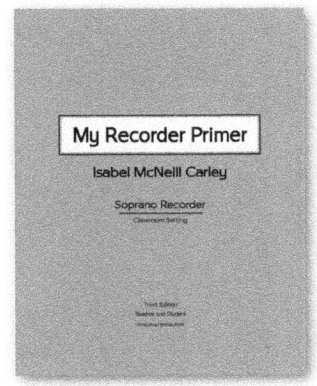 

Establish a secure musical foundation with the step-by-step lessons offered in **My Song Primer** (for singing) and **My Recorder Primer** (for soprano recorder). Songs are interwoven in lessons with speech and rhythm exercises, suggestions for percussion and Orff instruments, and ideas for games and movement.

13 Songs, one per lesson, from So-Mi to Pentatonic.
ISBN 978-0-9836545-4-4

35 Songs in 6 Lessons, D-E-G-A range.
ISBN 978-0-9836545-5-1

All new essays and articles plus a read-aloud story.
ISBN 978-0-9836545-9-9

Brasstown Press o brasstownpress@gmail.com o brasstownpress.com